TRAGEDY OF THE NEGRO

P. THOMAS STANFORD, M.A., M.D., D.D., LL.D.

THE TRAGEDY
OF THE NEGRO IN AMERICA

BY

P. THOMAS STANFORD

The Black Heritage Library Collection

BOOKS FOR LIBRARIES PRESS
FREEPORT, NEW YORK
1971

First Published 1897
Reprinted 1971

E185
S79

Reprinted from a copy in the
Fisk University Library Negro Collection

INTERNATIONAL STANDARD BOOK NUMBER:
0-8369-8932-5

LIBRARY OF CONGRESS CATALOG CARD NUMBER:
75-178483

PRINTED IN THE UNITED STATES OF AMERICA
BY
NEW WORLD BOOK MANUFACTURING CO., INC.
HALLANDALE, FLORIDA 33009

Second Edition. Tenth Thousand.

THE TRAGEDY

OF THE

NEGRO IN AMERICA

A CONDENSED HISTORY

OF THE

ENSLAVEMENT, SUFFERINGS, EMANCIPATION,
PRESENT CONDITION AND PROGRESS
OF THE NEGRO RACE IN THE UNITED
STATES OF AMERICA.

Prepared at the Special Request
of the Philanthropic Christian Public of
England and America, by

Rev. P. THOMAS STANFORD

A.M., M.D., D.D., LL.D.

Author of "FROM BONDAGE TO LIBERTY," "NEGRO HEROES AND HERO-
INES," etc., etc. President of New England Aid and Protective Associ-
ation for Friendless Colored Girls and Children, North Cam-
bridge, Mass. Contributor to the *Homiletic Review*,
London and New York. Vice President of Christ's
Medical and Theological College, Baltimore,
Maryland. Vice President of the National
Baptist Convention, Nashville, Tenn.

EDITOR'S EDITION.

101 AND 103 DUDLEY ST., NORTH CAMBRIDGE, MASS., U. S. A.
Where all Communications should be addressed.

163549

TO

MY MANY FRIENDS AND FELLOW-HELPERS

AND TO

ALL HONEST MEN WHO SYMPATHIZE WITH MY

RACE

I DEDICATE THIS SHORT STORY OF

NEGRO LIFE IN THE UNITED STATES, IN THE

HOPE OF HELPING CREATE A STRONG, HEALTHY

PUBLIC OPINION THAT WILL

MAKE IT IMPOSSIBLE FOR OUTRAGES AND LYNCHINGS

TO BE MUCH LONGER CONTINUED.

May, 1897.   P. T. S.

CONTENTS.

APPENDIX.

ILLUSTRATIONS.

ILLUSTRATIONS — (Continued).

PREFACE.

This volume is intended to compress, within the narrowest limits, an account of Negro life in the United States of America. I have consulted the most reliable histories, and made personal inquiries with great care, and can conscientiously present the story as trustworthy. No desire has been felt about gratifying the spirit of any race, but fairness to both white and black has been carefully kept in sight; the oppressors of the Negro have been looked at from every point of view in the hope of finding some excuse for their cruelty.

In my work as a Christian teacher I have naturally felt the deepest sympathy for the poor and needy, and devoted my chief care to them. I was born a slave, and lived for several years with the poorest of the poor, and can never forget my own poverty and sufferings; to help the down-trodden is a desire which never leaves me.

When the Public Meeting, which was held at the Wilberforce Memorial Church, Priestly Road, Birmingham, England, on the 28th of May, 1894, passed the following resolutions : —

" RESOLVED : That the Rev. Peter Stanford (England's Coloured Preacher) be deputed, in the interests of the philanthropic and Christian public of England, to visit the States for the purpose of investigating these alleged outrages, and of there pleading with the prominent white Christians to induce them to exert their influence in preventing further reprisals, and in insisting upon the enforcement of law and order."

" RESOLVED : That this meeting, having implicit confidence in the impartiality and good judgment as a representative of his race, hereby desires to assure the Rev. Peter Stanford of their entire sympathy and support " : — I felt there was nothing for me to do but relinquish my pastoral work in England, and as best I might proceed to discharge the new duties thrust upon me.

Leaving my Birmingham Church was the greatest trial of my life. Greater than the trials of my youth, because then I knew not the meaning of human sympathy and helpfulness ; greater than those of school and college days ; it was my greatest trial because the kindness and love of many friends must be left behind, could not longer be enjoyed in all the paths afforded by church fellowship, neither requited with gratitude in bodily presence. Until the day shall come that will witness my departure from this world, I can not forget the splendid generosity of my Birmingham Church members, and their sympathy in every time of trial will be enshrined in my heart.

When I arrived at America, and proceeded to
make investigation into the condition of my race,
I was soon convinced that a pamphlet of ten or a
dozen pages would not afford space enough for a
satisfactory description of it to be made; indeed,
were I to arrange, and print all the material now
in my possession a book several times the size of
this one would have to be issued. The history of
the Negro in America cannot yet be written; but
when it shall be written it will be a terrible comment on the character of many so-called Christians.
Pain, cruelty, and death will appear on almost
every page.

Having investigated as thoroughly as time, ability, and means permitted, the various outrages
reported in the press, and finding myself with
material enough for a large book, after much consideration and consultation with friends of my
race, I decided that a brief story of Negro life in
the States would best answer my purpose. I saw
that the outrages of to-day are merely repetitions
of previous outrages, the bad, poisonous fruit of
seed sown in the distant and near past, and was
convinced that the Negro's cause would be best
helped forward by a condensed statement of slave
history from the beginning. If I have successfully
compassed my intention, the reader will be able in
some measure to understand, at small expenditure

of money and time, the indescribable horrors of slavery, and see the fearful darkness in which my people lived for centuries, and in which millions of them now live.

To tell the story as effectually as possible, observations are made on Africa, and why and how the Negro was brought thence is explained; a few remarks are made respecting American geography and the founding of the States; John Brown, the puritan descendant who attempted to free the slaves, is described; what befell the Negro from 1619 to this present day is told in the briefest manner; Lynchings, which are so diabolically done until now, are set forth in the mildest possible language; some friends of the race are named with gratitude; the different conditions of the Negro of the North and his brother of the South are made as clear as the writers ability permits; and some suggestions are made for the consideration of all Christian people in respect of the future.

The attention of the reader is directed to the labour of the American Missionary Association among the coloured people of the South, of which it is impossible to speak with too much praise, and Tuskegee Normal and Industrial Institute, Alabama, Wilberforce University, Ohio, Guadalupe College, Texas, Hampton Normal and Industrial Institute, Virginia, Howard University, Washing-

ton, D. C., and Livingstone College, North Carolina, are mentioned gratefully, and brief descriptions
of the educational work they do are given. These
Christian and Educational Institutions will help
the Negro to attain a complete victory over all his
opponents.

Sending this "TRAGEDY OF THE NEGRO IN
AMERICA" — to me it *is* a tragedy — to the public,
I can not withold gratitude from any of the friends
who have helped me, but do thank one and all most
sincerely for the asssistance they have so willingly
rendered. Their reward must be my deepest thank-
fulness and, as I hope, an improved and healthier
public opinion on the Negro question.

Praying and hoping for God's blessing on this
poor effort to expose a perpetuated wrong and help
bring nearer the day of universal brotherhood, and
that He may send labourers, more and more, into
the "black malarial slough," and make them com-
petent to convey His love and enlightening spirit to
the millions of my race there living, I send it forth
in humility to do whatever of good is possible.

When I was called upon to write facts respecting the
condition of my people as they obtained both in the
Northern and Southern States of America, I accepted
with many misgivings as to how the public would
receive it and the good it might accomplish. I now
stand on this side of duty done, and have seen the book
pass into the hands of eager truth seekers in every walk

of life, who have showered me with letters, pulpit and press comments, of the highest commendation, and asking for another edition of *The Tragedy* and a Negro History, to be used in the public schools as a text-book. I feel deeply grateful and highly gratified.

Now, turning to my desk to respond to the call for another edition of my book, *The Tragedy*, I find myself confronted by more serious, intricate, and dangerous aspects of the Negro problem, which make me feel that it would be fair to my readers, many of whom may live under conditions which make it impossible for them to be eye witnesses of the Tragedy of the Negro in America, to place under the heading of Appendix matter gathered from the speeches and pens of others.

At the same time I am pushing ahead with the Negro History, and in a few weeks, God being my helper, I will place it at the service of our nation's children, who with outstretched hands and plaintive voices are clamoring for it.

                                              P. T. S.

COMMENTS

A FEW OF THE MANY PRESS COMMENTS, NAMES OF REVIEWERS AND INDORSERS OF DR. STANFORD'S WORK.

The Rev. P. Thomas Stanford, D.D., LL.D.,
Boston, Mass., U. S. A.
Dear Friend :—

I was glad when I learned that you had gone to the United States to make investigations respecting the present condition of your race. I know you to be willing and able to perform that important piece of work. As soon as your report is off the press send me a copy, and oblige,.

Yours faithfully,

W. E. GLADSTONE.

London, England, April 3, 1897.

Rev. P. T. Stanford, D.D., LL.D.,
Haverhill, Mass., U. S. A.
Dear Sir :

I thank you for a painfully interesting history. The device of lynching has been wonderful and horrible; its success would be still more so. We wait the issue with deep interest.

Yours very faithful,

W. E. GLADSTONE.

London, England, August 10, 1897.

Rev. P. Thomas Stanford, A.M., M.D., D.D., LL.D.,
Birmingham, England.

January 23, 1892.

Rev. and dear Brother :

During the last four years I have read with profound interest newspaper reports referring to you and your work in

Great Britain. I am proud of you because of your sterling worth and the able manner in which you have represented our race in high places among the world's leaders of men. I sincerely hope that many of the young men of our race will speedily copy your example. I am,

Yours truly,

FREDERICK DOUGLASS.

WASHINGTON, D. C.

———

The REV. P. THOS. STANFORD, D.D., LL.D.,
Haverhill, Mass.

July 23, 1897.

Dear Brother :—

I am past eighty years of age, and have given fifty years as a worker to the cause of your race. I stood shoulder to shoulder with my sister Harriet and brother Henry Ward in those dark days of slavery in defense of the negro race, and gathered much of the material for her *Uncle Tom's Cabin.* I am right glad to see from your ably written book, *The Tragedy of the Negro in America,* that the labors of my sister and brother were not spent upon you in vain, for truly their aim and ambition do show forth in you. Farewell, farewell. Be faithful.

Fraternally yours,

CHARLES BEECHER.

GEORGETOWN, MASS.

———

The REV. THOMAS STANFORD, A.M., M.D., D.D., LL.D.,
Boston, Mass.

Dear Sir :—

I have just finished reading your volume, *The Tragedy of the Negro in America.* I do not doubt that it is a true story of the tragical aspect of the negro's life in the United States, and that the truth of history requires that this should be told.

Yours truly,

LYMAN ABBOTT.

BROOKLYN, N. Y., December, 1897.

TUSKEGEE NORMAL AND INDUSTRIAL INSTITUTE—
INCORPORATED.

For the Training of Colored Young Men and Women.

TUSKEGEE, ALA., February 23, 1897.

REV. P. THOMAS STANFORD, D.D., LL.D.,
Boston, Mass.

My dear Brother :—

I assure you that we thank you kindly for this interest and help, and wish you much success in your forthcoming work, *The Tragedy of the Negro in America.*

Yours truly,

BOOKER T. WASHINGTON.

BOSTON, MASS., December, 1897.

To whom it may concern :—

Rev. P. Thomas Stanford, D.D., has served in the Garrison Memorial Church, a Home Missionary Church, in Boston, for more than a year. I gladly commend him to any people where, in the providence of God, his lot may be cast, as a man of irreproachable character, an able preacher, and a faithful pastor.

JOSHUA COIT,

Secretary Mass. Home Missionary Society.

Dr. P. Thomas Stanford is a brother whom I esteem and honor. He is in a peculiar position by reason of his race, history, his attainments and his standing both in this country and England, to do a peculiarly valuable work for both lands. His book, *The Tragedy of the Negro in America*, gives a true state of his race and deserves a world-wide circulation.

Faithfully yours,

FRANCIS E. CLARK,

President of the United Societies of the World's Christian Endeavorers.

BOSTON, MASS., 1890.

From SIR JAMES SAWYER, M.A., LL.D., KNT. F.R.C.P.,
M.D., F.R.S., D.P.
                                    10–12–02.

Dear Dr. Stanford: —

Many thanks for the *Afro-American* and for the *Colored American* magazine received to-day.

With hearty good wishes for Christmas,

JAMES SAWYER.

BIRMINGHAM, ENGLAND.

NORTHFIELD EXTENSION.

FOUNDED BY D. L. MOODY, 1897.

The officers of Christ Medical and Theological College, Baltimore, Md. : —

I am delighted that you have been able to secure the services of Rev. P. T. Stanford, D.D. It is now fifteen years since I first made his acquaintance on the other side of the Atlantic, where it was my privilege to come into very close personal friendship and co-operation with him. All I knew of him endeared me to him as a brother in Christ and in the ministry of His Word.

With best wishes for all future blessing upon the College and people, I am,

Yours in the bonds of the gospel,

G. CAMPBELL MORGAN.

BALTIMORE, February 14, 1902.

IN APPRECIATION OF A NOBLE WORK.

The following letter from Rev. Alexander McKenzie, D.D., pastor of the First Congregational Church, Cambridge, has been received by Rev. Dr. P. Thomas Stanford, the founder and president of the Massachusetts Aid and Protective Association for Friendless Colored Girls, North Cambridge, whose noble work among the unfortunate of his race has been indorsed by President McKinley and many of the most prominent men of the State.—*The Transcript.*

CAMBRIDGE, March 22, 1900.

My dear Dr. Stanford :—

I thank you for your book, which I have read with painful interest. You have told the sad tale in strong terms. I am glad you could state also the more hopeful signs. It cannot be long that these outrages last. Your race has had a fearful history in this country, but there has been improvement, and this will continue. Cherish your hope, and keep on in your good work. I shall be glad to say anything I can to further the cause to which you are devoted. I have also read your excellent sermon; you put much thought into small compass. The sermon should be of service among the thoughtful people, and all others can feel the force of your argument. You do not ask for aid, but I venture to inclose a small check to help your work in North Cambridge.

Yours very truly,

ALEXANDER McKENZIE.

CHARITY + LODGE, + No. + 1551.

MASONIC HALL, NEW STREET, BIRMINGHAM. *England*

This is to Certify to all whom it may concern, that our worthy Brother _Rev^d P Thomas Stanford, M.d, D.D, LL_ who was _Inhaled At_ on the _Fifteenth_ day of _May_ A.D. _1894_, Resigned on the _Feb First_ day of _February_, A.D. _1895_, and has paid all dues up to that date. Signed this _10^th_ day of _October 1902_

_____Worshipful Master.

L. Holder, Treasurer.

H Upton acting Secretary.

EXTRACTS FROM PRESS COMMENTS.

"Rev. Dr. P. Thomas Stanford, who at the special request of the British public is about to go to America, his native home, to investigate the condition of his people there, has lived here about fifteen years. The doctor was born in slavery and came here to study. His conduct as a student, lecturer, and preacher has won for him the respect and high appreciation of Her Majesty the Queen, His Royal Highness the Prince of Wales, and the personal friendship and help of the Rt. Hon. W. E. Gladstone."—*London Daily Graphic*, February 3, 1890.

"In Birmingham, England, there is a congregation which is white that for eight years had a black preacher. This learned and distinguished preacher is the Rev. P. Thomas Stanford, M.A., M.D., D.D., LL.D., who is now doing work among his own people here in America."—*The Christian Educator*, November, 1896.

"As a scholar, educator, and Christian gentleman, Rev. P. Thomas Stanford, M.A., M.D., D.D., LL.D., stands foremost among his race."—*Daily Herald*, Boston, September, 1891.

"Dr. P. Thomas Stanford, who for several years officiated in our city as pastor, and was known as England's Colored Minister, and was sent to America in 1894 to report upon the condition of his people, has just published the record of his work in volume form under the title of *The Tragedy of the Negro in America*, which in our opinion is equal to and calculated to do as much as Mrs. Harriet Beecher Stowe's *Uncle Tom's Cabin*."—*Daily Gazette*, Birmingham, England, August 6, 1897.

"Rev. P. Thomas Stanford, President of the New England Aid and Protective Association for Indigent Negro Girls and Children, has been laboring successfully among the poor and neglected of his people in Boston and vicinity for some eight years, has been called recently to divide his time with Baltimore as preacher, lecturer and teacher. The great number of his

people who help to populate that great city numbering over one
hundred thousand offers a rare opportunity for the doctor to
display his world-acknowledged ability as a ripe scholar, an able
preacher, and faithful representative of his race."—*The Transcript*, Boston, December, 1902.

"Rev. P. Thomas Stanford, M.A., M.D., D.D., LL.D., late
pastor of Calvary Baptist Temple of Baltimore, Md., who has
just been elected Vice President of Christ Medical and Theological College of that great city, though born a slave forty years
ago, is to-day one of the most scholarly men of the race. He
studied medicine, law and theology, both in this country and
England. He was educated through the efforts of Rev. Henry
Ward Beecher and Mrs. Harriet Beecher Stowe, and the Rt.
Hón. William E. Gladstone."—*The Boston Guardian*, November 8, 1902.

The Tragedy of the Negro in America. By Rev. P. Thomas
Stanford, D.D., LL.D. Illustrated, 12mo., cloth. Author's
edition.

To tell the story of the negro people in this country is to go
back over a long period of time and to chronicle many vicissi-
tudes of fortune. Dr. Stanford, lately pastor of the Wilberforce
Memorial Church, Birmingham, England, is now engaged in
work for his fellow colored people in the New England Aid and
Protective Association for Friendless Colored Girls and Children,
North Cambridge, and other parts of America, and is here profit-
ing by the wide experience and study given by him in the past to
the elevation of the negro. He has consulted the most reliable
histories and has made personal inquiries with great care, and can
conscientiously present his story as trustworthy. Dr. Stanford
speaks with great earnestness and conviction, and it is certain
that his outline of the negro's status in this country from the
earliest times to the present will clear up mistaken notions in
many minds, and give many new ideas of the black man's place
in our body politic. No desire has been felt about gratifying the
spirit of any one race, but in the writing of the book fairness to
both white and black has been studiously kept in sight.—*Cambridge Chronicle*.

NOVEMBER 4, 1899.

Rev. Dr. P. T. Stanford has written *The Tragedy of the Negro in America.* Apparently he was sent to this country from England, where he used to be pastor of the Wilberforce Memorial Church in Birmingham, for the purpose of studying the treatment of the colored race to which he belongs, and of writing an account of it for English readers. This book offers a condensed history of the enslavement, sufferings, emancipation, present condition and progress of the Negro race in the United States. This announced purpose is fulfilled in a commendable degree, and it does what it attempts to do in a readable fashion, and it contains many facts of significance, and its moral deductions and conclusions are heartily to be approved. It will help to promote a healthy public sentiment, and to create a more kindly and righteous spirit toward the colored race wherever there is need thereof.—*The Congregationalist.*

BOSTON, MASS., September 9, 1897.

NOTES AND COMMENTS ON
DR. STANFORD'S SCHOOL HISTORY.

WANTS NEGRO HISTORY USED.

[BOSTON TRAVELER, February 12, 1903.]

Rev. P. Thomas Stanford, M.A., M.D., D.D., LL.D., a learned and distinguished colored writer, is in the public eye at present as an advocate of a movement to eradicate the prejudice against the negro by introducing into the history of the country, as taught in the public schools, a series of articles dealing with the good that the negro race has done, to offset the popular opinion of his race while they were in slavery.

Dr. Stanford is president of the New England Aid and Protective Association for Friendless Girls and Children at Cambridge, and vice president of Christ's Medical and Theological College at Baltimore, Md.

Dr. Stanford aims to correct to a certain extent the prevalent view taken by the public concerning the supposed inferiority of the negro as a nation. He insists that the public should consider the black man as a hero, not as a slave, or a descendant of slaves.

AMERICAN UNITARIAN ASSOCIATION,
25 Beacon Street, Boston, Mass.
February 26, 1903.

I believe that Dr. Stanford has a most valuable plan in hand. Rightly carried out, such a book as he intends to produce will enlighten the rising generation, spread correct historical views, dispel prejudices, and advance the cause of the negro. Education in the home and school is the great agency of modern civilization. I wish all success to this publication.

(Signed)   EDWARD E. HORTON,
President of Unitarian Sunday-school Society of America.

IGNORANCE AND PREJUDICE.

To the Editor Boston Traveler :—

During the last two weeks I have been more than ordinarily interested in the letters which have appeared in your "People's

Column " from the pens of our people. You have awakened an interest in the colored citizens of Boston which is unusual, because, as a rule, they are not given to reading the newspapers, and the reason is because most of them are filling such servile positions that when they are released they are so tired that an attempt to read would be fruitless. All of the letters show that each writer fully grasps the texts given them by you, even down to the little girl who wrote; but of them all I think the one by Rev. P. Thomas Stanford, M.A., M.D., D.D., LL.D., dealt with the subject most masterly. The doctor has not only diagnosed the case, but suggested a remedy. You say he " wants negro history used." Ignorance is a great evil, and is, no doubt, the cause of the race prejudice in our country.

From time immemorial it has been human nature to applaud the brave, the true and loyal, and that these qualities are to be found in the negro's character are facts which stand out in bold relief in true American history. Dr. Stanford understands the situation of the case, and as a sociologist knows how to treat the malady. We all know that in order to bring about a reformation in matters socially between the white and colored people of this land, the nation must be taken hold of while in childhood. To do this a better method has yet to be found than the one suggested by Dr. Stanford, and God grant that the history of our race by him will soon be found in every schoolroom in our land.

Thanking you for the interest you take in our cause, I am a constant reader of the *Traveler* and an old school-teacher.

Yours truly, E. M. W.

Somerville, Mass., February 24, 1903.

At the instance of His Eminence James Cardinal Gibbons,
408 North Charles Street,
Baltimore, Md.

February 4, 1903.

Rev. P. Thos. Stanford, M.A., M.D., D.D., LL.D.

Dear Sir:—

I am desired by the cardinal to thank you for your very kind words, which he appreciates.

He will be pleased to review your book.

Yours truly,

(Signed) WM. T. RUSSELL, *Sec'y.*

Rev. F. B. Meyer, B. A.,
Christ Church, London, England.

February 18, 1903.

DR. STANFORD, Boston, Mass., U. S. A.,
Vice President of Christ Medical and Theological College,
Baltimore, Md.

Dear Sir :—
I shall be glad to see you when you come to London.

Yours sincerely,

F. B. MEYER.

FROM A LITTLE GIRL.

To the Editor Boston Traveler :—

I hope you will pardon me, being only a little girl, for writing to you about the letters that you had in your paper about our colored people. All of us children like them very much. We colored children who go to the North Cambridge schools were glad to see our Dr. Stanford's picture in your paper Wednesday night, and to know that he has written a history about our big men and women who are dead. We are going to ask our teachers to let us have his book in the schools alongside of our United States histories. For really, Mr. Editor, I am ashamed of the names that we are called in the history, " slaves and niggers," and when we read that part of it the white children look at us real funny. I know Dr. Stanford will tell them better in his book. Won't you please help us to tease the teachers to let us have his book as well as other books in our schools? Please put this in your paper for me.

BEATRICE (age 12 years).

NORTH CAMBRIDGE, MASS., February 16, 1903.

The school board of Cambridge, Mass., selects facts respecting the lives of great men and their work, and has the teachers talk about them to their classes one afternoon in the month. These schools are mixed with colored and white children. Last Friday the life and work of Rev. P. Thomas Stanford, D.D., LL.D., President of the Massachusetts Aid and Protective Association for Indigent Colored Girls and Children, of Cambridge, was the subject.—*Afro-American Ledger.*

BALTIMORE, March 8, 1902.

Lynch Law and the Negro.

T a Public Meeting held at the Wilberforce Memorial Church, Priestley Road, Birmingham, May 28th, 1894, the following action was taken :—

Having heard, with deep pain and regret, representations made by newspapers and otherwise as to the *Treatment to which the Coloured Race is Subjected* at the hands of some of the white citizens of the *Southern portion of the United States of America*—

Resolved —" That the Rev. PETER STANFORD (England's Coloured Preacher) be deputed, in the interests of the philanthropic and Christian public of England, to visit the States for the purpose of investigating these alleged outrages, and of there pleading with the prominent white Christians to induce them to exert their influence in preventing further reprisals, and in insisting upon the enforcement of law and order

Resolved —" That this meeting, having implicit confidence in the impartiality and good judgment, as a representative of his race, hereby desire to assure the Rev. PETER STANFORD of their entire sympathy and support."

Moved by Mr. ROBERT NIXON, City Councillor, Chairman; Seconded by Mr. ALBERT EDWARD ARTHUR, Deacon.

(Signed),   A. D. EKINS, *Church Secretary.*
G. BOWEN LLOYD, *Church Financial Secretary.*

Rev. Peter Stanford, England's Coloured Minister.

The following are a few of the leading men in England who have attached their signatures to the above, and who fully sympathise with the noble and arduous Mission undertaken by the Rev. PETER STANFORD :—

Sir JAMES SAWYER, Knt., F.R.C.P., M.D., Lond., F.R.S, Edin., J.P.
City Alderman WILLIAM WHITE, J.P., Birmingham
City Alderman WILLIAM COOK, J.P., Birmingham.
City Alderman A. BAKER, J.P., Birmingham.
City Alderman R. C. BARROW, J.P., Birmingham.
City Alderman SAMUEL EDWARDS, Birmingham.
City Alderman FREDERICK BALLAH, Birmingham.
County Councillor JOSEPH MALINS, G.C.T., Worcestershire.
City Councillor SAMUEL LLOYD, J.P., Birmingham,
City Councillor ELI BLOOR, J.P., Birmingham.
City Councillor WHEELER HAINES, M.R.C.S., Birmingham.
City Councillor SAMUEL E. JOHNSON, M.R.C.S., Birmingham.
City Councillor GEO. EDWARD STEMBRIDGE, Birmingham.
City Councillor THOMAS ARTER, Birmingham.
City Councillor R. F. MARTINEAU, Birmingham.
City Councillor W. J. LANCASTER, Birmingham.
City Councillor JOHN V. STEVENS, Birmingham.
City Councillor G. H. JOHNSTONE, Birmingham.
City Councillor JOHN KIMBERLEY, Birmingham,
City Councillor R. C. JARVIS, Birmingham.
City Councillor J. JACOBS, J.P., Birmingham.
Rev. JOHN O. WEST, B.A., Vicar of St. Matthew's, Birmingham.
Rev. G. N. H. TREDENNICK, M.A., Vicar of Sparkbrook, Birmingham.
Rev. W. HEAD, M.A., Brilley Vicarage, Whitney-on-Wye, late of Birmingham
Rev. JOHN CLIFFORD, M.A., D.D., LL.B., B.Sc., F.G.S., Baptist, London.
Rev. CHARLES JOSEPH, Baptist, Southsea, late of Birmingham.
Rev. EVAN LEWIS, Baptist, Hay, Brecon.
Rev. GEORGE DUNNETT, Baptist Minister, Coseley.
Rev. WILLIAM H BISHOP, Baptist Minister, King's Heath.
Rev. N. M HENNESSEY, Congregational Minister, Birmingham.
Rev. W. O. ASTBURY, Congregational Minister, Birmingham.
Rev. T. TRAVERS SHERLOCK, B.A., Congregational Minister, Smethwick, Birmingham.
Rev. J NICHOLAS KNIGHT, Congregational Minister, Birmingham.
Rev. GEORGE CAMPBELL MORGAN, Congregational Minister, Birmingham.

Rev. THOMAS CARTER, Minister of the Presbyterian Church of England, Birmingham.
Rev. W. EWING, Minister of the Presbyterian Church of England, Birmingham.
Rev. W. PEDLEY, Methodist, Birmingham.
Rev. E. S. COLE, Primitive Methodist Minister, Birmingham.
Rev J S. WHITE, Primitive Methodist Minister, Birmingham.
Rev. HENRY JAMES, Methodist New Connexion, Birmingham.
Rev. F. W. BOURNE, Bible Christian Minister, London.
Rev. R. R. RODGERS, Wretham Road Church, Birmingham.
Rev. W. J. CLARKE, Hurst Street Church, Birmingham.
Captain JOHN HILLARY, Salvation Army, Citadel, Birmingham.
Captain EDWARD TEMPERTON, Salvation Army, Green.
RICHARD CADBURY, Esq., J.P., Birmingham.
J. FRANCIS BRAME, Esq., J.P., ex-Vice U.S. Consul, Birmingham.
J. A. LANGFORD, Esq., LL.D., Birmingham.
EDWARD C. ANDERSON, Esq., M.A., M.D., Birmingham.
HUGO YOUNG, Esq., M.A., Barrister-at-Law, Birmingham.
J. J. PARFITT, Esq., B.A., Barrister-at-Law, Birmingham.
E. J. STANBURY EARDLEY, Esq., Counsel-at-Law.
ARTHUR T. CARR, Esq., Ph.B., F.R.H.S., Solicitor.
GEORGE B. WILSON, B.A., Solicitor, Birmingham.
EDWARD BICKLEY, Esq., Solicitor, Birmingham.
T. C. LOWE, Esq., B.A., Birmingham.
HENRY WHITWELL, Esq., Secretary Y.M.C.A., Birmingham.
J. B. COLLINGS, Esq., Editor "Good Templars' Watchword."
R. J. BUCKLEY, Esq., Author of "Ireland as it is."
WILLIAM ADAMS, Esq., Superintendent Refuge Assurance Co.
JOHN LAWSON, Esq., Secretary Band of Hope Union.
JOSHUA MOSELEY, Esq., Secretary U.K. Alliance.
GEORGE ORMAN, Esq., Secretary of the Sunday Closing Association for Midland Counties.
WILLIAM LEWIS NEWEY, Esq., F.S.A.A., F.S.S., Birmingham.
JAMES ALLEN, Esq., F.S.S.C., Birmingham.
JAMES MOFFAT, Esq., Contractor, Birmingham.
EDWARD CROSS, Esq., F.G.S., Birmingham.
WILLIAM HOWE, Esq., Clerk of Christ Church, Sparkbrook.
JOSEPH GEORGE PENTLAND, Highgate Road, Sparkbrook, Birmingham.

The Appointment of Mr. STANFORD has been endorsed and confirmed at a number of Churches and Public Meetings all over the country, and further endorsements are being received daily.

Financial Committee—

HERBERT E. CARR, Esq. *(Chairman)*, J. RYAN-BELL, Esq, Mr. JOSEPH LOCKETT, Mr. A. D. EKINS, Mr. W ROBINS, Mr. PETER STANFORD, Mr. G. BOWEN LLOYD, Mr. HENRY J. CROSS, Mr. J. G. PENTLAND.

Hon. Accountants :—MESSRS. CARR AND LOCKETT, 6 and 8, County Chambers, Corporation Street, Birmingham.

Hon. Treasurer :—J. RYAN-BELL, Esq.

Hon. Secretary of the Committee :—MR. A. D. EKINS, 337, Balsall Heath Road, Birmingham, England, to whom all communications are to be addressed. [Hon. Private Secretary to the Rev. PETER STANFORD, MR. G. BOWEN LLOYD.]

☞ Donations may be forwarded to the Hon. Treasurer, J. RYAN-BELL, Esq., Lloyds Bank, Stratford Road, Birmingham, and will be acknowledged by the Hon. Secretary.

CHIEF OFFICES OF THE COMMITTEE: 6 & 8, COUNTY CHAMBERS, CORPORATION STREET, BIRMINGHAM.

Mr. Stanford leaves England last week in September.

MRS. HARRIET BEECHER STOWE,
AUTHOR OF "UNCLE TOM'S CABIN."

CHAPTER I.

Loss of life by unauthorized violence, and the resulting unhappiness to others, is called a tragedy; and, every tragedy of real life has stimulated the best and the worst passions of mankind to vigorous interest and exertion. All tragedies, however, have not been caused by unauthorized violence; the pages of history are black with records of the foulest crimes, of violations of human rights and the divine law, by violence *authorized* and made *legal* by men in whom power was vested.

The history of the Martyrs of England, France, and Spain is a tragedy which began in the distant past, whose pains and horrors, which were the direct result of misuse of power by cruel kings and bigoted statesmen, were realized by men and women of many generations; and, in this day of civilization and advanced knowledge of christianity, the world is looking with weary eyes and sickened heart upon a tragedy in Armenia, commanded and made legal by the Sultan of Turkey, in which little children

3

are mutilated, helpless women are outraged, and unarmed toiling men are horribly done to death. This is an *authorized*, not an unauthorized, tragedy, which the whole world knows, but has not yet been outraged enough to stop it ; more cruelties must be done and more human blood must flow before the Christian powers will be sufficiently stimulated to dethrone the murderer and restore peace and order to the fairest garden of the east. "Come and see the works of God : " said one of old, "His eyes behold the nations : let not the rebellious exalt themselves." "To me belongeth vengeance, and recompense ; their foot shall slide in due time : for the day of their calamity is at hand, and the things that shall come upon them make haste." Man knows not as God knows ; sees not as He sees. It is written, however, so that he who runs may read, that all tyrants shall fall ; all cruelties will be avenged ; all powers which brutalize mankind must be either saved by fire or destroyed ; the righteousness of God is ordained to prevail in the world ; and, the brotherhood of man shall be fully established.

In America, — which is known as the land of the free, whose people are rightly proud of a history that speaks of a noble, victorious struggle against tyranny ; of the wisdom, foresight, and piety of the founders of the States ; of the marvellous energy which transformed vast plains and forests into fields of wealth creating grain and fruit, built cities, established manufactures, and made a large sphere of art and science ; — a long and revolting tragedy has been in progress, in which the Negro has suffered indescribable misery and been afflicted with diabolical torture. This also was a tragedy *authorized* by the powers that were, was recognized and defined by law, and endorsed and supported by not a few churches and religious teachers, in which the Negro was bound with chains, whipped with the lash, treated as a beast, sold in the common market as a thing, and, when he was no longer worth money, hurried to death and buried anyhow.

This *authorized* tragedy came to an end ; by fire, the fire of the vengeance of righteousness, it was destroyed. In the great conflagration of the War of Emancipation, which would not have happened had the United States of America been willing to know God's will without pain and blood-shed, no preserving angel walked to keep those from harm and death who were engaged therein ; the *nation* had sinned, and could not be relieved from sin's penalty. The nation paid the penalty in money and in blood, and thereby saved herself from the fate of Babylon, Assyria, and Rome. Nations that forget God and forsake righteousness cannot abide ; they have been, and will be, overthrown. Power cannot forever stay in the hand of the tyrant ; prosperity forsakes

the land of blood ; ignorance and every debasing
habit are the heritage of nations that do wickedly ;
decay and destruction wait for the people who
oppress the poor. This authorized tragedy of the
States, whose sufferer was the poor Negro, was
always abhorred by pious men and righteous citizens, and eventually aroused the natural good
feeling of the multitude, who together swept it
away and prevented the country from sliding into
immeasurable disgrace and calamity.

The *authorized* tragedy of the Negro in America,
then, ended in a pouring out of blood and of treasure, and in a vast war tax which continues until
now ; but did not in its death struggle engulf all
the meanness of iniquity. They who fought against
emancipation, and many who fought for emancipation, when the war was over and the Negro set free,
were unwilling, and remain unwilling, to recognize
in him a brother. He was free ; let him care for
himself, and see what he could make of his freedom.
Free, it is true, but untaught, homeless, moneyless,
a stranger in a land whose people loved him not.
Free ; yes, free ; to look on the fields he had made
smile with harvests, but not to call one grain of the
wheat his own ; to gaze with what intelligence was
in him on all the wealth he had created, but not to
find one copper of it in his own pocket ; to behold
luxury and affluence all around him, but not to

have a home for himself, in which to find shelter, peace, and love. History tells of men being cast on uninhabited islands, in which naught but trees and wild fruit grew; in which birds lived and reared their young, and wild beasts prowled and fought each other; which was an unfortunate experience. But they were free to fell the trees and make houses of wood for themselves, and to pluck the wild fruit and catch the fish of the streams for food, and to use the implements of defence they possessed in their struggle with the beasts; and more than once have men filled desolate parts of the earth with human life, prosperity, peace, and happiness by merely putting forth unhindered effort. How much worse was the position of the emancipated Negro than that of ship-wrecked men cast on uninhabited, fruitful islands!

The authorized Negro tragedy in the United States of America did indeed come to an end, but the *unauthorized* tragedy began with the declaration of emancipation; and, had there been no righteousness therein, no hearts of flesh, no men whose souls had received the light of God and the compassion which is tender and eternal, the poor coloured man must have wished, had he known of such a thing, that he might be free as the ship-wrecked mariner to pluck and eat wild fruit in a lonely land, and make for himself a home out of wood which no man

claimed. Land there was around him in the States,
stretching away in every direction, thousands of
miles of it, but none of it his; he must ask per-
mission of the owners to live on it, which fact kept
him in their power, and enabled the unworthy to
continue the tragedy in an unauthorized form,
which continues until now. Will it forever continue? Let men who deny the Negro equal opportunity, who say equal civic rights are enough for
him, who hinder and obstruct his development and
progress in every imaginable manner, who cast him
out of the sphere of white men and lynch him to
death on the smallest provocation, remember the
saying : — "He that oppresseth the poor reproach-
eth his Maker." It may be that a few bold, bad men
live, in whom neither faith nor love dwells, who
dare even reproach God, who will do so until the
grave swallow them up, and persecute not Negroes
only, but whom they can of any colour; but it can
not be that the enlightened United States will forever tolerate this unauthorized tragedy of the Negro,
this unlawful lynching which occurs in so many
places. Yet a little while, and, surely, the righteous
people of the States will once more make an effort,
an effort of peace, in the name of "Our Father who
art in heaven," to make it impossible in their
country for child of His to suffer hardship because
of colour, and bring to an end the reproach of caste
which rests now on black and white equally.

It is the purpose of this little book, which pretends only to be a report of inquiries made, to present in brief form the history of the Negro from the time of his importation into America as an article of commerce down to this day. The writer aims not at sensation, but desires first to see for himself the facts in their true light, and, having seen, give to his readers an unexaggerated statement thereof. No cause is assisted by falsehood; no race of men can be permanently helped forward by fraud. The scriptures are as full of warnings against misrepresentation, as against oppression, and all human history affords for all who are willing to see the clearest demonstrations of how falsehood developes destruction. Not by falsehood, then, does this book seek to promote the Negro's cause, but by a simple and brief story of his life in America. It may be that white men and black men will never be as one people, perhaps cannot be; but none who have accepted the teachings of the Christ can refuse to accord equal opportunity to the sons of Africa.

MRS. HARRIET BEECHER STOWE'S HOUSE,
IN WHICH SHE WROTE "UNCLE TOM'S CABIN."

CHAPTER II.

Africa, an immense peninsula of the Old World,
the third in size of the great divisions of the globe,
is a land of ignorance and darkness, and the home
of the Negro. "Its greatest length is about 5,000
miles ; its greatest breadth is about 4,600 miles ; its
superficial area comprises nearly 12,000,000 square
miles ; its population is estimated at 200,000,000."
Fifty years ago this vast peninsula was a land of
mystery, of which we had the most meagre maps,
and of whose people we knew next to nothing.

The Phœnicians, who lived in cities on the coast
of Syria, one of which was ancient Tyre, were
devoted to the pursuit of the sea, and established
colonies on the north coast of Africa, and created
extensive commerce. It is said of them that they
were the first people to circumnavigate Africa, and
that Necho, who ascended the throne of Egypt in
the year 617, B.C. was the navigator. The Carthaginians, who established a mighty empire, and

absorbed all the Phœnician settlements of the West, followed in the steps of the Phœnicians, and sent their navy along the Atlantic Shores of Africa, which returned in the year 570, B.C., having settled several colonies on the coast. Herodotus, who was born in the year 484, B.C., was the first Greek who travelled in quest of distant lands and the founder of Grecian geography. He explored Egypt as far as the Cataracts of the Nile, and made excursions into Lybia and Arabia, and subsequently wrote accurate descriptions of the countries he visited. After Herodotus, little seems to have been written of Africa until Ptolemy, — who was born in Egypt and lived in the second century of the Christian Era,— wrote his " Universal Geography, illustrated with maps, which was not superseded as the text book of science till the fifteenth century." After Ptolemy, nobody wrote much of Africa, and little is known of that strange land, other than that provided by the Phœnicians, Carthaginians, Herodotus, and Ptolemy, until modern maritime discovery began in the fifteenth century, after which information was afforded that astonished the world. Since then adventurers, explorers, and missionaries have been busy in the great work of discovering the world, and of bringing to those in darkness the light of the truth of God. Adventurers went forth in ships, which were paid for in their own money, to gain wealth ; explorers, to make discovery in the name of king and country for the benefit of both ; missionaries, to declare the knowledge and love of the Most High. Adventurers left behind them the bitterness of cruelty and the devastation of greed ; explorers made it easier for mankind to understand the greatness of the earth ; missionaries advanced, and yet advance, the eternal good of the human race by displaying before untaught men the gentleness and sympathy of the Christ. The age of the adventurer in its ancient form is ended, passed and gone forever, and can never return in its old, bad sense of theft and murder ; but the humane explorer and the Christian missionary possess both present and future, in which they may together pursue their beneficent work.

The Portuguese, who explored the West coast of Africa in the fifteenth century, and the Spaniards, who gained possession of South America, were the first Christian powers that paid attention to Africa, and did indeed erect the figure of the Cross there, and upon every new land they discovered ; but by their foul and brutal practices caused the holy symbol to remind the native tribes of rapine and murder. They respected no right of property in the land, in the produce of the country, not even in the flesh and blood of the natives ; but treated all and sundry with indignity and plunder. They have long since received the recoiling punishment of wrong doing, and are to-day among the weakest and poorest nations of the world.

Africa, whose peoples, it must be said, have inflicted fearful cruelties upon one another, has not escaped the ravages of the adventurer; but when her true history shall be written, the names of Mungo Park, Dr. Barth, Dr. Livingstone, Dr. Moffat, Mr. Stanley, and a host of others will stand out in letters of gold for all time, and the African of the future, who will certainly be educated and one day stand erect among men, claiming and receiving perfect equality, will in them recognize under the providence of God, the saviours of his race. Then, in his native land of luxuriant vegetation, fruitful fields, noble rivers, vast forests, and immense deposits of mineral wealth, and wherever else he may chance to live or be, white men will respect him, and none will dare speak of slavery, shackles or death.

Man is one the whole world over, and consists of a single species. He is distinguished from the animals beneath him by conscience, reason, and speech, and is so marvellously endowed that he can adapt himself to every known climate. His intelligence has taught him how to protect himself from the cold of the North, and to endure the heat of the South. He may be found in every climate, from

the hottest to the coldest.   In vast forests, in regions
of fertility, in wastes of sterility, in valleys and in
mountains he finds a home, and makes the earth
provide him food and shelter.   But man is not the
same in stature, intelligence, and colour in every
place ; diversity obtains most prominently ; but
colour is the most noticeable feature of difference.
His skin is black, yellow, olive, tawny, white, but
he is man, qualified for the highest effort of mind and
the holiest act of worship.   Whether black or white,
educated or uneducated, he is the same creature in
his feelings, and has ideas of a state after death, of
a supreme power, of guilt, of pardon, which vary
according to his state of enlightenment.   The saying that God " hath made of one blood all nations
of men for to dwell on all the face of the earth " has
been abundantly established as a truism all over
the world, particularly by the rising of several
savage tribes to the average level of educated
nations.   The ancestry of mankind is one ancestry,
and man everywhere is the child of a divine father,
and is destined for an eternal life, and nations ought
to cultivate sentiments of peace and good-will.   It
is the duty of the learned to teach the unlearned ;
the strong to help the weak ; and, they who have
knowledge of God and are conscious of His sus-
taining grace and love are under the heaviest
obligation to rescue from wretchedness, guilt, and

impurity those who are ignorant and depraved, that the identity of man be perfect.

If this be true ; if men ought to respect and help each other, and recognize before God their common origin and the obligation resting upon each to promote the good of all ; — of which in this day there can be no doubt — the question, how the Negro was brought from Africa to America, and why, becomes very interesting, particularly so in view of the conditions of his past and present state therein. In the answer we shall see how strangely events of life intertwine with each other.

In the year 1485, just seven years before Columbus was permitted by Ferdinand and Isabella of Spain to sail westward in search of unknown lands, who discovered Watling Island, one of the Bahamas, and one of the great islands of Cuba and St. Domingo, Alfonso de Aviso discovered Benin, Africa, which then comprised Benin, Dahomey, and Yoruba, three Negro kingdoms, and subsequently Fernando Po of Portugal established a Portuguese Colony and the Church of Rome at Gaton, Benin. The Brothers of Jesus laboured in their usual manner to convert the natives to Christianity, to Christianity as they understood it; but met with small success. Knowing not the "perseverance of the gospel," and not being qualified to labour in patience and love they adopted a quicker

method of conversion than that of the Master.
They turned their attention to the king, who cared
little for their new religion, but much for the satis-
fying of his personal desires. This untaught son
of the Dark Continent made a proposition, viz.,
that he would turn Christian, and compel his subjects also to turn, if the Brothers of Jesus would
find him a white wife. He asked for a white wife
to be provided as he would for any article of manu-
facture that was new to him, and probably was not
conscious of any existing difference between a piece
of cloth and a wife ; but the same cannot be said of
the Brothers of Jesus. However, knowing or not
knowing that marriage is a sacred covenant, they
agreed to the king's proposal, and forthwith proceeded to keep their part of the agreement. They
went to the Sisters of St. Thomas, an order of women
devoted to charity and holy work, and, wonderful
to relate, one of the Sisters consented to accept the
king as husband. What prompted her to agree to
this extraordinary compact ? Human love was out
of the question, because she had never seen him,
and it is difficult to imagine that any lower desire
moved her. Let it be written down to the eternal
credit of this nameless Sister of Mercy that she
placed her all on the altar of sacrifice in the name of
the Son of Man. Nothing more is heard of her ; but
her noble effort, — noble from her point of view —

though probably successful for a time, failed of a permanent settlement of Christianity in the king's country. Why? The Portuguese established the slave trade in Gaton, which is answer enough. Men cannot preach the Kingdom of God, establish colonies in peace, prosperity and social order, and at the same time buy and sell, or steal and sell, flesh and blood. "Ye can not serve God and Mammon." It is impossible to educate and civilize the human race by any such self-destructive method; piety and holiness can not be preached by men who traffic in human life.

The influence of this diabolical conduct of the Portuguese was almost instantaneous on the natives, who, taught by the evil example of the Europeans, themselves became man stealers and followers of the slave trade. Then the poor, ignorant people, who had previously tilled the land and pursued the calling of fishermen, gave themselves to the work of hell, and carried all who were weaker than they to the coast, and for the merest trifles, for worthless trinkets, sold them into slavery. This was the white man's work in Benin. Instead of inspiring honesty, truthfulness and gentleness, he stirred up a huge sea of treachery, duplicity and cruelty, and made himself rich for a time by the proceeds of miseries immeasurable which were heaped on the helpless, the aged, and all who were unable to pro-

tect themselves. He can find no excuse for his base
conduct in the cruelty of the King of Dahomey, the
adjoining kingdom, whose court was paved with
human skulls, and whose palace, — the place he
called his palace — walls were decorated in like manner. There it stands, and will abide, a deep black
mark of infamy against the white man, who went
to Africa to establish colonies and preach heaven,
yet managed to create pandemonium on earth.

This fiendish work was begun by white men on
the coast of Africa between the years 1485 and 1490,
and in 1492 Columbus set forth to find lands in the
West. Following Columbus, but unlike Columbus, were thousands of Spaniards, and legendary
stories of the measureless wealth of the West were
soon told far and wide. Spain was then preemi-
nent among the nations of the world, and pointed
with pride to continents discovered by her mariners.
But Spain was unfitted to be the missionary of
heaven; she was drunk with the lust of gold, knew
not liberty, gloried in her cruel inquisition, and has
long since found her reward. Other nations entered
into the work of discovery, and wrested from her
the supremacy. On the fifth of March, 1496, John
Cabot was commissioned by Henry VII. of England
"to sail into eastern, western, or northern seas with
a fleet of five ships, to search for islands, provinces
and regions hitherto unseen by Christian people,

and to set up the banners of England on city, island, country or continent, and, as vassal of the English Crown, to possess and occupy the territories which might be found." On the twenty-fourth of June, 1497, fourteen months after Columbus on his third voyage came in sight of the main land, John Cabot discovered the Western Continent, and, "having sailed three hundred leagues along the coast, planted on the land the flag of England." Then followed in due time Sir Walter Raleigh, Sir Richard Grenville, Cavendish, the great navigator, and ultimately the Pilgrim Fathers, and English colonies were established in Virginia and in Massachusetts. In 1664 the English defeated the Dutch at New York, and became the masters of North America.

In that wonderful fifteenth century, then, we find the Portuguese in Africa, the Spaniard in South America, the Dutch in New York, the English in Virginia, and subsequently in Massachusetts. White winged ships crossed and re-crossed every sea, carrying cargoes of commerce to favourable ports. Why not carry cargoes of Negroes? Were there not enough and to spare of them in Africa? Had not the Portuguese stolen and sold them in 1485? It was a profitable idea; not to be forgotten. They were black men, therefore inferior, fit only to obey the white man, who needed them to

do the work of the New World. The Dutch of
New York would buy some Negroes, or steal them;
would sell them and make money; and, in 1619, a
Dutch Man of War brought the first slaves, fourteen
in number, to Virginia. There the captain of the
ship gave them in exchange for provisions to
Captain Miles Kendall, deputy-governor of the
colony. Why not? In those days few men so
much as thought of the great sin which was being
committed, and were utterly incapable of foreseeing
the fearful heritage of sorrow that would accrue to
succeeding generations. This is *how* the Negro
was brought from Africa. First by the Dutch, in a
Man of War, and the *why* may be seen in the money
value of so much free labour, which was made to
produce harvests at the low cost af feeding.

To look back on those fearless Englishmen, who
fought like heroes in defence of their own homes
and country, and laboured continuously that wife
and child might be fed and clothed, and supplied
with every comfort the earth could produce, and see
them doing the devil's work so shamelessly, is to
look upon a scene which causes infinite regret,
which more than suggests the thought that England's priests had grossly neglected to guide rightly
her valiant men. The Dutch, too, were brave and
religious, thrifty and careful of each other, yet
could barter in flesh and blood, which proves how

strangely and awfully both good and evil are mixed in man. Love of money, a real, frightful source of wrong in all times, blinded the eyes of these brave men, and prevented them seeing rightly; and, having no prophet to warn and guide them, they fell into the blackest sin. For money and ease of life they gave play to the worst passions of human nature, and dared heaven, perhaps unconsciously, to curse them, which curse came then and there, though they knew it not, and burst in tornadoes of of fire, shot and death on succeeding generations.

We see, then, *how* and *why* the Negro was brought from Africa to America, and it is known that this mad trafficing in blood, which stained the banners of England and America, finally cost both countries millions of treasure and thousands of lives to erase the blot. It is a tragedy indeed, this of the Negro in America, which we are watching, on which also a silent, offended God looks; but a tragedy whose end is not death to all concerned; a tragedy whose clearest fact is fire, the fire of cleansing and deliverance. It is strange that men will so depart from virtue and plunge so deeply into sin, when they know that catastrophe must follow. Meanwhile, we leave white and black men face to face, one the owner and oppressor, the other the owned and oppressed, and will see in following chapters how the mighty battle was fought and won between right and wrong.

MRS. HARRIET TUBMAN.

SHE ACTED AS A SPY FOR THE UNION ARMY.

CHAPTER III.

The geography and history of the United States
need not more than a passing glance ; the Negro
and what has befallen him therein being the subject of this little book.   It is enough to say that
the territory of the States stretches for thousands
of miles in every direction, that the population
exceeds the huge figure of 70,000,000, and that for
great rivers, coal fields, gold mines, silver mines
and agriculture it is not surpassed by any other
part of the globe.   The growth of its population is
one of the world's wonders ; a kind of miracle
wrought by steam boat and railroad train.   In the
year 1800 it amounted to about 6,000,000, that is, it
was not more than the population of London to-day ;
had increased to 39,000,000 at the census of 1870,
and, — an extraordinary fact — as stated above, to
70,000,000 at this present time.   The natural leaders
of this great population, which is composed of men
from almost every nation under the sun, have rest-

ing upon them a responsibility that will not be
easily borne, a responsibility which calls for the
highest qualities of mind, extensive knowledge of
human nature, and faith in the providence of God.

Compared with the older nations of Europe and
Asia, the States are yet in their infancy; but have
in the short period of one hundred years become
infinitely more important than most of them in
respect of everything pertaining to the good of the
human family. Here are Greeks, Russians, Ar-
menians, Germans, French, Chinese, Japanese,
English, Irish, Scotch and Americans, men born
under every form of government and trained in con-
flicting ideas of religion and morals, bound together
in a free republican government, each having the
right to vote in City, State and National affairs. It
has been an experiment, perhaps is so yet, in human
government on a vast scale; but appearances justify
the remark that it has successfully stood the test
of trial, and that to-day, thanks to Washington,
Adams, Webster, Lincoln, and many other noble
men, who devoted extraordinary powers of mind to
the service of the New Nation, is better established
than many of the dynasties of the Old World.

But the States were not a nation of 70,000,000 of
inhabitants when white and black man first stood
face to face on American soil; they were colonies of
England, and were governed by that extraordinary

power, which has so marvellously colonized so
many portions of the globe. But the England of
the year 1619, when those fourteen slaves were
landed on the shore of Virginia, and given in
exchange for provisions to Captain Miles Kendall,
deputy-governor of that state, and the England of
to-day are scarcely comparable. Then, it is true,
Englishmen were free men, and could pursue the
calling of their choice in perfect safety; but the
toiling millions were practically outside of the constitution, and had no voice whatever in the government of the country. Then England was governed
by the aristocrasy and the free-holders, who formed
a very small part of the population, and the colonies
were in the hands of chartered trading companies.
Corruption was in every office; the House of Commons was in the power of the House of Lords; seats
in the Commons were bought and sold openly, and
places of power were given without regard to merit;
reformers, men who sought the privilege of the
vote, were persecuted and even put to death by the
sword; and, not until the year 1832 was the constitution widened so as to admit persons of substantial
position, which good work was completed in 1867
with Household Suffrage. To-day it is a different
and better England. Every working man who has
a home or a lodging can vote in every election that
is held, whether for City Counsellors, Members of

School Board, Members of the House of Commons, or any representative position, and can even be elected himself. Corruption is dead; the power of the House of Lords is small, and cannot be exercised at all in respect of money bills; seats in the Commons are no longer, cannot be, bought and sold; places of power are bestowed according to merit and length of service; reformers are free to advocate reform in open meeting or in any manner not harmful to the persons and property of the inhabitants, without fear of interference. To-day, as some one has well put it: — "England is a republic with a hereditary president" and protects her citizens the wide world over, and suffers no slave to live beneath her banner.

Let England and America, then, as we know them to-day, be in no sense blamed for the *fixing* of a slave-system in the States. Both countries have paid in money and in blood the price of the sin of dead generations, and are the greatest hope of mankind. In a holy rivalry they hold up the torch of civilizing light, spread on every hand the beneficence of business, display before all nations the safety and solidity of national life based in the free vote of their peoples, and send forth missionaries at immense cost to all who are in the darkness of ignorance. Personal wrong there surely is in both countries, which is inflicted by individuals upon

others who can not help themselves ; but the wisdom
of their peoples and rulers will yet find a remedy for
these evils, and perfection will be attained as nearly
as is possible in human institutions. In that good
time which is certainly before both countries, the
unworthy effort of many wicked persons to place
the Negro outside the human family will be finally
defeated, and race prejudice in the States will be
dead.

Returning to the evil year 1619, we find that
Captain Butler succeeded Captain Miles Kendall in
the governorship of Virginia, and that a disgraceful
dispute arose respecting the ownership of the fourteen slaves. He claimed the negroes in the name
of the Earl of Warwick which claim Captain Miles
Kendall resisted, and sought what he called equity
by placing his case before the London company.
From the beginning of the traffic, human strife and
cruelty were alarmingly aggravated, and men of all
stations in life were filled with the meanest wickedness, rich and poor alike, from the Earl of Warwick
to the poorest black man who was strong enough
to kid-nap a weaker black man and sell him into
slavery on the coast. This dispute was not quickly
settled. However, in July, 1622, the London Court
disposed of the case, giving nine slaves to Captain
Kendall and the remainder to the company. But
what is the terrible fact of this fixing of the slave

system in the States? This: That the English colony of Virginia purchased the first Negroes who were brought to the States, and inaugurated the hideous traffic in human flesh and blood. For this most shameful act of inhumanity, out of which crime too black and foul to be described grew, the reader must not blame either England or America; it was the act of men who had left the Old Country to seek wealth and get it in any manner, righteous or unrighteous, who scrupled not to class a man with a coloured skin with the beasts of the field. Their reward is shame, which clings to them until now, and reflects disastrously upon the otherwise fair fame of the wisest and best of them.

The institution of slavery, once established, took root, but did not grow rapidly. Taking the census of the colony of Virginia of February 16, 1624, the fourteen slaves of 1619 had only grown to twenty-two. Perhaps they were a little afraid of the system; may be conscience troubled many of the colonists; or, what is quite as likely, importers of flesh and blood were probably not over well supplied by Negro stealers. But twenty-four years subsequently, in 1648, the population of Virginia was about 15,000, of whom 300 were slaves. Evidently the whites had somewhat lost fear of the system in those twenty-four years, if they ever felt it, and it is equally certain that conscience had been *educated*.

The colonists of 1648 were not a reputable lot; indeed there were more men of bad character among them than the original settlers and their descendants liked. Thieves, vagrants, burglars and disorderly persons of every evil character, who had been sent to Virginia by the English Government for their crimes at home, formed no inconsiderable part of the population ; yet were more graciously received than the poor Negro. It is difficult, if not impossible, in this day of enlightenment to imagine how a God-fearing man, — many of the colonists were such — could bring himself to treat a condemned criminal with greater kindness than he was willing to extend to a Negro ; yet such is one of the ugly facts of that time. Sin is subtle, and overthrows the best of men, if they cease to fight it, and destroys their manhood, covers them with disgrace, and causes them to make the most ignoble laws. It so happened in Virginia. On September 17, 1630, an act of prohibition was passed by the colonists to the following effect : " That the banished criminals of England must not have relations with Negroes." Think of it. The vilest of the vile, men too bad to be allowed a place in English life, banished for offences proven against them in courts of law, must not defile themselves with the Negro ! Language, it is said, undergoes perpetual enlargement of meaning and purification, and it must be true that defile-

ment could not have meant in Virginia at the time
now under consideration what it means to-day.
How *could* a criminal, a creature of the blackest
indecencies, defile himself by having relations with
an ignorant, untaught, probably trustful Negro?
The defilement would be more on the side of the
Negro, though he knew it not.   Yet the prohibition
was made, and the punishment for every such offence
was public flogging and confession of the offence in
church on the following sabbath.   Bad men may
make bad laws, and other bad men will break them,
even as good laws are broken, and have been broken
in every age.

The colonists had to bring out the whip and hear
confession in church ; villany could not forego the
easy prey within its reach.   Hugh Davis, a white
servant, whose name is written in history forever, —
whether an English criminal or an ordinary colonist
we know not — was indeed publicly flogged before
a company of blacks and whites for defiling himself
with a Negro.   He was not the last victim of this
vicious law ; but if it were possible or right to sympathize with a worker of iniquity, Hugh Davis
would have our sympathy.   We *can pity* him, and
regret that he could defile himself with any child of
God ; but for the Negro, whose education along
lines of debasement, cunning and treachery had
been continued by white men, only *sympathy* ought

to be felt. He was a natural child of the forest, acquainted with the rudest life only, knowing nothing of civilization and little of the white man, whose whole subsequent history in America would have been different and better had he been put to work in a humane manner and treated as a man who needed training in skilled labour and educating in letters. It was not. Therefore, he became the cause, by no fault of his own, of the most fearful struggle of modern times, which held in suspense for four years the very life of a mighty nation, whose salvation was accomplished by the slaughter of 1,000,000 men.

From 1619 until 1662 slavery existed without any direct sanction in law, and had no foundation in the order of state Virginia, the mother state of slavery, and none in any other state. It was a case of one man owning another because he had bought him. But was he not property? He had cost money. Slave owners felt the need of a law, which would fix beyond dispute the right of ownership, as real estate was fixed, and on the fourteenth of December, 1662, the foundations of slavery were laid by a proclamation — "that the issue of slave mothers should follow their condition." No help now for the Negro, neither for any innocent child born of a coloured mother; for two hundred years he must toil, bleed, die in the service of the white man, and not dare to murmur. For two hundred years he must obey his master and ask no questions, though he hear questions of right and wrong discussed. Patience must be the order of his tribe ; ignorance and suffering *will* abide with him. While this inhuman business was being done, it is certain that Christian mothers in Virginia taught their children that stealing, swearing, speaking falsely, coveting another's property and committing adultery were all sins against God and man ; and, it is equally certain that so-called Christian fathers did steal the Negro's labour, did most cruelly abuse him, did commit adultery with their own slaves with the horrid intent of increasing their live stock, and forsook, turned their backs upon every feeling of humanity. God has made it easy for man in all the departments of morality to decide the right and the wrong, in view of which eternal fact no excuse can be found for slave owners. They decided, those original slave owners of Virginia, "that the issue of slave mothers should follow their condition," and thereby accomplished two things ; viz, hereditary slavery, and statutary sanction thereof. Thus far this battle between right and wrong went against right in the person and life of the Negro, and the quotations given below will show how tightly the manacles were fastened to his feet and hands.

In 1670, Virginia, thoroughly accustomed to the

infamous institution, and having realized the profit
of so much unpaid labour, declared by Act of
Assembly that " all servants not Christians, coming
into the colony by shipping, should be slaves for
their lives."

On the twenty-fourth of October, 1684, the prov-
ince of New York made the slave trade legitimate
within its borders, recognizing that the white man
had a right to buy and sell the coloured man.

On the fourth of October, 1705, an act was passed
without a single dissenting voice, declaring the
Negro, Mulatto and Indian, slaves within their
dominion.

In 1706 an act was passed to "encourage the
baptism of Negroes," which was done, it is said,
"to quiet the public mind on the question."

On the thirty-first of October, 1751, King George
II. issued a proclamation repealing the act which
declared slaves real estate.

Thus the business went, all against the Negro,
who had become a thing. King George II. declared
he must not be "real estate," but left him to be
classed with cattle, or crops, or any other miserable
article, and the traffic increased. In 1648 there
were 300 slaves in the colony of Virginia; in 1671
— 2,000; in 1715 — 23,000; and in 1758 more than
100,000, which was only a little less than the white
population. Think of it. In one hundred and

thirty-nine years fourteen slaves had increased to
over 100,000; an awful fact, which caused even
Virginia to realize that the institution was a most
serious and alarming one. True, it was a well
organized system, and recognized in the most solemn
manner by the law; was defended by the Church of
Christ, the Church of Him who declared and revealed the brotherhood of man, and Christian ministers received slaves as salary; yet was the ghost
that haunted the vision of many good men, and a
problem which was ultimately solved by a volcanic
upheaval that scattered death on every hand.   It
was futile to baptize the Negro that his soul might
be saved ; that same Negro lived and multiplied to
baptize a nation in blood.   He had no rights; could
not appear as witness in any court of law; could be
condemned on the evidence of one witness without
a jury; could own nothing; if he secretly saved
anything it was taken from him; had no family
relations such as white men enjoyed; lived together
by common consent; dared not strike a Christian
or Jew, no matter what the provocation; had no
schools; was at last buried in a common ditch.
Pity 'tis there was no prophet in those days to fore-
see coming events, and to warn men of judgment to
come.   Such an one might have saved past and
present generations from deep disgrace and exhaust-
ing strife.

This is what befell the Negro in the States of America between the years 1619 and 1712. God, it is said, never makes haste, but that His will is certain of execution. We do know that He desires none to be ignorant, and that He seeks to save every child of man with a complete salvation. With Him was the issue, and is, and as we shall examine and describe the condition of the Negro from 1712 to 1865, the year of emancipation, — his life on the plantations, his struggles for freedom, his simple, hearty acceptance of the gospel, his glad awakening on the day of redemption, and his most wonderful subsequent progress, we shall hope to see that the hand of God is set against the wrong doing of men, and behold the promise, set as in rainbow-light and beauty, "that the kingdoms of this world" *shall* "become the kingdoms of God and His Christ."

HON. FREDERICK DOUGLASS.
THE NEGRO STATESMAN AND ORATOR.

CHAPTER IV.

HOW THE NEGRO WAS TREATED DOWN TO 1844.

The closing years of the nineteenth century will be looked back upon by future generations with considerable interest, and the whole century will be esteemed the most important in results of beneficence to human life since the time of Jesus Christ. Man has always been king of all creatures living on earth; but time never was when he stood for so much as now. Fortune, caste, privilege and birth, the historic barrier builders, are by no means passed and done with, yet do not obstruct individual progress so seriously as they used to; there is now plenty of room for earnest capable men to exercise their personal powers. Vast business companies and combinations notwithstanding, which certainly many times and in different ways destroy the best efforts of the individual, a man of energy, endowed with faith in the Almighty, may make much of his life. Christian sympathy and the spirit of God are his assistants, by whose help he may overcome many difficulties. Indeed, the fact is, whenever

we see success of any kind we know that a man is
behind it, though we see him not.   Ideas, principles,
truth and right are indispensible, it is true; but
until a living man incarnates them, and puts them
into active operation, not much is accomplished.
A man of noble personality, — who loves truth, dis-
penses right, lives by principle, does right because it
is right and refuses to do wrong because it is wrong,
and disseminates ideas of holiness, — inspires everybody and moves hundreds forward to the ground
of hope and a happier existence.   Such an one, —
possessing a tender conscience, natural piety, a
glowing heart full of sympathy and benevolence,
and a high moral purpose in all he does — carries
heaven with him and strengthens the weakness of
all among whom he moves.   Jesus Christ, Martin
Luther, John Knox and John Wesley; Tennyson,
Longfellow and Whittier; Thos. Carlyle, Emerson
and Chas. Dickens were men who saw, and knew,
and taught, and the whole civilized world looks back
upon them with admiration and gratitude.   Jesus
Christ was the incomparable one, who illumined
human consciousness and commenced an era of
never ending progress, whose name must always
be mentioned with reverence.   When men listen to
His teaching and emulate His example it is well for
the world, and progress is advanced in the best and
surest manner.   If dead generations had walked in

His footsteps, obeying His commands, and if living generations were eager above all things to keep His law, slavery had never been amongst men in the last nineteen centuries, and war and standing armies would have no place in the life of nations to-day.

Looking back from this wonderful nineteenth century to the year 1712, in which the Negro in the States of America found himself bound by manacles of slavery, in which, also, men and women, the men and women who owned him, feared God and reverenced Jesus Christ, it is difficult to realize that the holy name had much influence with them, and no one could for a moment believe that it had if evidence were not abundantly at hand in proof thereof. " They feared God and worshipped their idols " was said by one of old of a well known people, which saying might with perfect justice be applied to many of the original slave owners.   It seems mysterious that the year, in which the Dutch man of war landed the first batch of slaves at Jamestown, Virginia, bore the "Mayflower" to the New World, whose passengers were men and women that sought a new home and liberty to worship God according to their conscience.   The "Mayflower" carried a freight of piety, learning and Christian civilization which were to be written into the law of the New World; the Dutch man of war carried a burden of wretchedness and sorrow, and a system destined to perish in the flames its own hand should kindle. The Pilgrim Fathers were men whose fame has gone forth over all the world, and probably to the end of time they will be held up as ensamples of robust faith, fearless courage, and sincere piety; yet it is certain that slavery was established in Massachusetts not long after their arrival. Chief-Justice Parsons declared from the bench that "slavery was introduced into Massachusetts soon after its first settlement and was tolerated until the ratification of the present constitution of 1780." Let all ministers of the gospel observe this fact, and be it their duty never to weaken God's demand for righteousness. Need there is for real prophets, who seek not wealth, neither position, who will at any cost warn men of the sinfulness of sin. Slavery cannot come back, but other evils are here, and will increase in power and in destructiveness, if the voice of the preacher be not true to the solemn duty of declaring the whole counsel of God.

The first mention of Negroes in Massachusetts we find in the year 1633. It appears that some Indians found a creature in the woods they thought was the devil, of whom they were so afraid that they dared neither approach nor touch him. They hastened to the English settlers, and declared they had seen the evil spirit. The English returned with the terrified red men to the woods and found a harmless black man, who was lost, had wandered from his master's house ; but they sent him back to his master. Why? Why did they not keep him, and instruct him in their religion, and in all useful social duties? He was a black man, and was owned by a white man, which is explanation enough. It was no doubt honest to send him back ; but it would have been more in keeping with the religion they professed to have kept and treated him in a Christian manner. This amusing incident of red men being afraid of a black man, and of white men returning him to his owner on a point of honesty, brings into clearest view the peculiar, soul-saddening fact, that religious people can be morally blind and do grossly immoral acts.

Who the owner was of this solitary Negro is not known, neither does history tell how he came into Massachusetts; but it is clearly recorded that the first importation of slaves into the state was in 1637, just four years after the above mentioned event, who were brought from Barbados, and for whom Indians were given in exchange.

At first, slavery in Massachusetts, as in the other colonies, was a family business, which was its most harmless form ; then it became an affair of the community ; and, finally, an ordinary business of men who wished to enjoy the fruits of forced labour.

Like all the works of sin it developed into larger
proportions, destroyed the humanity of men, and
filled the colonies with unworthiness. In 1720,
General Shute placed the number of slaves in
Massachusetts, including a few Indians, at 2,000.
In 1735 there were 2,600, and within the next
seventeen years the Negro population of Boston
alone was 1,541. In 1754 a system of taxation was
established by the Colonial government, which
included black people in the schedule of taxable
property, not a little to the confusion of Governor
Shirley. In his message of November 19, 1754, to
the assembly, he said : "There is one part of the
estate, viz., the Negro slaves, which I am at a loss
how to come at the knowledge of, without your
assistance." But he was helped out of his difficulty.
In that year 4,489 Negroes were classed with hogs,
and in 1764 the number had increased to 5,779.
5,779 human beings, in Massachusetts, the home of
the Pilgrim Fathers, were rated with hogs and
horses, and Negro children were considered an in-
cumbrance, and were given away like puppy dogs.

It is impossible to believe that all the Colonists
countenanced this horrible business, indeed it is
certain they did not ; but it is clear that the life of
the colony was morally poisoned, which was the
unhappy condition of all the English colonies in
the year 1754, Georgia excepted. The natural

rights of thousands were subverted. They were "deemed, held, taken, reputed and adjudged in law to be chattels personal to all interests, constructions and purposes whatsoever," as the law put it ; which was contrary to reason and the admonitions of conscience, and gratified the spirit of vulgar pride and class distinction, and the lust of dominion. Violence was the spirit of slavery, and depraved greed its inspiration. From the first slave-hunt in unhappy Africa to the surrender of General Lee at Appomattox, its blood-stained hand was laid on the bodies and souls of the slaves, and on the moral sensibilities of the people. It had no mercy ; knew no decency ; forced the slave to make the earth produce harvests ; whipped him ; sold him ; killed him ; defied God and the inexorable law of righteousness. But Jehovah's judgment came at last in the awful War of Emancipation, and men trembled ; and, let this never be forgotten, all who thus disobey must, either here or yonder, in time or eternity, stand in the same sure retribution. It was the old sin, of which many are guilty to-day, of "doing wrong that good may come." There is nothing before men who forget righteousness but confusion and disaster.

It is with astonishment we read the state papers and official documents bearing on the slave trade ; they cause us to imagine that we hear the clanking chains which bound living men to a living death; but when to-day we see 8,000,000 of Negroes living and toiling as free men a great hope is felt, which is related to the whole Negro race in Africa and America. May not these 8,000,000, when they shall have won equality as well as liberty, provide our missionary societies the best ministers for the African field? Is it impossible for them to become a power under the providence of God which shall lift the entire race of coloured people to conditions of moral and spiritual life? They have suffered, and yet suffer. They have been in the blackest darkness of despair; but now see a light of hope, in which thousands of them rejoice perfectly. They have been, as their brethren in Africa are to-day, untaught, savage and immoral; but are now gaining knowledge, and becoming followers of Christ. All their suffering and degradation, heroic struggles and present pursuit of things worthy and sacred cannot end merely in their own elevation, but must surely have some relation to the uplifting of the race.

It has puzzled and perplexed thoughtful men to explain the connection between suffering and progress, and probably no satisfactory solution of the problem has yet been found; but it is known that the cleansing fire of affliction and the noblest character have a close relation with each other.

There is something in prolonged prosperity which demoralizes most men, and something in fierce adversity that draws the grandest soul-elements to the surface. The man who never had a personal Gethsemane knows not the supremest glory of the Mount of Transfiguration; the greatest men and women have braved the storm. Is it not possible, then, that what men call the worst thing may turn out the best? The undisciplined soul cannot be compared with the soul that has by bitter experience learned the deepest truth of the Christ. The Negro, therefore, may yet, by the over-ruling providence of God, become one of the world's most noble benefactors. While we follow to a close the history of his life in America, this hope of future extensive good shall be cherished, and faith reposed in God.

Resuming the story of his life in the United States of America, a quotation from the pen of the immortal Rev. George Whitefield, the renowned evangelist, who travelled extensively through the Southern States, will help the reader to understand the awful sufferings that were inflicted upon him. "In 1739, Mr. Whitefield said, in a letter he addressed to the inhabitants of the Southern States, that his sympathies had been strongly excited by what he had seen of the 'miseries of the poor Negroes.' He called attention to the practice of slave-masters, and the encouragement it afforded to the savage

tribes in Africa to continue their warfare on each
other, to supply the demand for slaves thus created.
He charged 'the generality' of them with using
their slaves 'as bad as though they were brutes;
nay, worse,'—worse than their horses which were
'fed and properly cared for' after the labours of the
day, while the slaves must grind their corn and
prepare their own food, — worse than their dogs,
who are 'caressed and fondled' while the slaves
'are scarce permitted to pick up the crumbs which
fall from their master's table.' He spoke of the
cruel lashings which 'ploughed their backs and
made long furrows,' sometimes ending in death.
He reminded them of their spacious houses and
sumptuous fare ; while they to whose 'indefatigable
labours' their luxuries were 'owing had neither
convenient food to eat nor proper raiment to put
on.' '' Mr. Whitefield did not exaggerate ; but
placed on record a faithful description of what he
had seen, which record can not be destroyed. His
letter briefly set forth what was happening in all
the English colonies, Georgia excepted. In New
Hampshire, Massachusetts, Rhode Island, Connec-
ticut, New York, New Jersey, Pennsylvania, Dela-
ware, Maryland, Virginia, North Carolina, and
South Carolina, in one degree or another of fiendishness, more severely in some states than others,
these cruelties were inflicted on 58,850 human

beings, each one a sensitive creature, capable of feeling pain, and endowed with faculties of soul, whose deep moan and uttered cry for deliverance went up constantly to heaven.

It is impossible to set forth in words the horrors of the trade in New York. The Dutch, under whose government it was known as New Netherlands, looked on slavery as a necessary evil, but did not treat slaves with cruelty. They added them to their families, taught them letters as best they could, and called them in to family prayers; but bought and sold them in the ordinary manner. When the Dutch were defeated by the English the lot of the Negro changed for the worse; a system of neglect, punishment and torture was introduced. In 1702 the assembly passed a law which was called "An Act for Regulating Slaves," and the following quotations show the quality of that regulation. It was declared "not lawful to trade with Negro slaves;" "not more than three slaves may meet together;" "a slave must not strike a freeman;" "all the children of freed black mothers already born, or yet to be born, must be slaves;" "that a common whipper be appointed." No lion in his cage, no eagle fastened by chain to post, fed and cared for by keeper, was ever so miserable as the poor Negro in the bad past. He might walk about and work; but no Christian or Jew would risk fine and im-

prisonment by trading with him.   He was allowed
to talk with two other Negroes; but if more than
three met together they were all whipped by a J. P.
or the common whipper, or sent to jail.   A freeman
was at liberty to beat him anywhere and anyhow;
but let him so much as raise his hand in self-
defence, and legal punishment followed.   A *freed*
black woman — some of the better sort gave manu-
mission papers to their slaves — could become a
mother; but her child was taken from her as soon
as he could work and was pushed into slavery,
often sold to a dealer in another state.   All this
being true, how great ought one's sympathy to be
for coloured men and women who are the children
of parents that were so ill-treated!   That they can
believe in a God of righteousness, that they do not
hate and abhor the white man, is the miracle of our
time, and a solid proof of the divine that is in them.

From the eleventh of May to the twenty-ninth of
August, 1741, — only three short months — one
hundred and fifty slaves were cast into prison in
New York; eighteen of whom were hanged, fourteen burnt to death, seventy-one transported to other
colonies, — sold for cash — and the remainder, forty-
seven of them, pardoned.   For what?   Absolutely
nothing.   One, Mary Barton by name, gave out a
report that the slaves had made a plot to burn the
town and murder the inhabitants, which was absurd

on the face of it. Yet Justices lost their heads, and the inhabitants, each one armed, — slaves were unarmed — became terror stricken, and hanging and burning were done without mercy. "The wicked fleeth, when no man pursueth."

God is the maker and judge of all men. He made us innocent, and never placed burden on mortal man beyond his strength, nor imposed a duty that could not be discharged; but men have created apparently inexplicable contradictions, crooked aspirations, and injustice and impurity, and now and again vainly endeavour to run away from their own badness.

Looking steadfastly into this Egyptian darkness of slavery in the States we see a little light of promise; and, in God-fearing men, most of them Quakers, such as Leister King, Elizur Wright, John Sloane of Ravenna, David Hudson, from whom Hudson City received its name, and Owen Brown, father of the immortal John Brown, we discern His ambassadors, who feared not to proclaim their Master's will. They did not labour in vain. As early as 1726, the Colonists of Virginia, alarmed by the increase of slaves, tried to check further importation by imposing a tax; but "the African company obtained the repeal of that law." In 1760, South Carolina endeavoured to restrict the traffic, "for which she received the rebuke of the British government.'' Earlier than the Colonists of Virginia, the people of Pennsylvania passed a law in 1712 to prevent the increase of slaves, which the Crown promptly annulled. In 1771, also in 1774, Massachusetts adopted measures for the abolition of slavery; but the Colonial Governors, who represented the government, refused to approve them, and so they were lost. Rhode Island, more fortunate than the other colonies, passed a law in 1774, prohibiting the importation of slaves, and in 1784, declared all children free born after the next March, of which acts the government took no notice. Light was breaking through the clouds; this was the first step towards emancipation. No more slaves to be imported, and all children of slaves then in the state, also all children to be born, to be free, meant the redemption of Rhode Island from the horrible crime, and had more influence in the other states than can now be measured.

The light and the promise grow more clear while we look, and circumstances of good omen accumulate. With the annexation of Texas, a vast country adapted to the growth of cotton, which increased the demand for and the price of slaves, we see a bolder activity on the part of the Quakers, who, filled with the love of God and man, stepped forth before all men to render aid to the hunted fugitive. The hunted fugitive? Yes; for the slave had at

last found manhood enough in himself to attempt
escape, to fly from the auction block, the flesh and
blood jobbers, the pain of the lash and the woe of
children sent from his heart into other lands. To
Eastern Pennsylvania hundreds of them took flight,
and were received and helped by good Samaritans.
This was the beginning of the end. God had
assisted the Negro to feel his manhood, and had
provided good men to help him. The slave power
might, and did, continue to oppress him; deny him
the rights of citizenship; prohibit meetings and
schools; forbid him to preach to his brother slaves;
punish white men who dared to instruct him; bind
manacles tighter to his feet; but in vain. He had
learned that men lived in other places who were
ready to serve him, and had discovered a personal
courage to dare something for himself. Previous
to the annexation of Texas came the revolution,
and separation from England, in which the Negro
found that he could use arms, and was encouraged
by both Colonists and Crown to do so, and of 501,102
slaves at that time in the States, some fought for
the Crown and some for the Colonists. They knew
not for what they fought; but it was a new experience, and was not forgotten.

His valour, however, did not win liberty for him.
After the new constitution had been ratified, and
the States were established as a separate nation, he

went back to his labour and sorrow; for him no
improvement had been won. But something had
been won personal to himself, which was increased
courage and bolder daring. He had seen white
men fight for something they called liberty; had
ignorantly fought with them, and had seen many
new things. And slaves in every state had heard
of Canada, a land far away; but of distance they
knew nothing and cared less. With miraculous
courage and wonderful faith thousands of them
ventured forth; were helped by a society known as
the Underground Railroad; — composed of good
men of all creeds — were fed and directed; were
sheltered by day and conducted through the woods
by night; and, it is pleasing to read that they
always proffered to pay in labour for what they had
received. The light grows clearer, and thousands
of men are looking at the horrid cruelties of darkness, and much earnest discussion is heard throughout the land.

It is 1844, just two hundred and twenty-five years
since those unfortunate fourteen slaves were delivered to the Governor of Virginia, and the divine
judgment of slavery and slave-holders is getting
nearer. In eighteen years the inhabitants of the
States will know what slavery means, and how fearful a thing it is to forsake righteousness. England,
once a partner in the business, has meanwhile made

a noble repentance, and has set free every slave that lived beneath her banner, and never more will stain her hands with the blood of such a crime. More than that; at her own cost and as best she can she prevents the crime being committed by others. Her sons of to-day must not be blamed for the sins of their fathers.   But in 1844 the darkness had not passed from the United States, though thousands of her noblest sons saw the light, and sorrowed o'er the sin ; the storm might not be avoided, but must break in death-giving force upon them.   The Negro must suffer and wear his manacles yet a while. Then the world shall see and the States *feel* the awful judgment of God, and widows will weep, and sons lament, and fathers moan for those who are not.

JOHN BROWN.
PURITAN HERO, CHRISTIAN PHILOSOPHER, MARTYR
FOR THE SLAVES.

CHAPTER V.

JOHN BROWN.

On the seventeenth of October, 1859, John Brown, at the head of a small force of armed men, entered the town of Harper's Ferry, Virginia, a little after ten o'clock in the evening, to free the slaves. Five coloured and fourteen white men constituted the entire force, with which he hoped not to destroy the huge slave party of the South, but to create a feeling, or so inflame a feeling already created, that would burn in Christian hearts until the power of that party should be destroyed. He took possession of the armoury buildings, cut the telegraph wires, stopped trains on the railroad, liberated several slaves, and held the town not much longer than a day. The slave party, at first, were astounded, if not for a moment paralized; then they laughed, and said : '' The folly of a madman.'' John Brown could not with his small force accomplish a task which ultimately cost millions of treasure and one million lives ; but he could, and did, reveal to the anti-slave party, as they had never seen it before,

the evil spirit of the slave party in its diabolical
nature and purpose.

On the nineteenth of October, 1859, only two days
after his bold attack on the town, John Brown was
cast into prison, where he remained until the seventh
of November without a change of clothing, and,
his wounds not withstanding, without medical aid;
and, forty-two days from the time of his imprisonment was hanged to death.   The raid, capture, trial,
conviction and execution of this wonderful man
and his followers profoundly stirred the nation, and
attracted the attention of the civilized nations of the
world.   His friends, who admired his simplicity of
heart and life, felt very sorrowful; thought he had
made a grievous mistake and that military action
would not advance legitimate reform; the slave-
owners were excited and furiously determined to
stand by their *property*.   But his friends did not
know that they had opposed to them the worst,
most wicked, subtlest of sin-serving men this world
has ever seen; they could not then feel, for which
they cannot be blamed, that only blood and death
could rid the nation of the evil of slavery.   But it
was brought home to them a few months after John
Brown's execution, when they saw for the first
time that it was war or eternal disgrace, perhaps
destruction.   Then all good men of every creed,
with infinite regret, but with courage made mighty

by burning indignation, drew the sword, not to sheath it until the curse was destroyed.

We are, always have been, for peace, and must oppose war; but if ever war was justifiable, that of the emancipation is justified. It was not desired by the North, the government did not seek it, there was no coveted territory to be won, not a private interest to be advanced; it was a case of wresting from blood-stained hands that would not peaceably let go millions of human beings.

John Brown did not mean war; but was mysteriously, no doubt providentially, influenced at the last moment to depart from his original plan. To quote from a letter he wrote on the fifteenth of November, 1859, to a minister of religion, it is clear that some influence moved him to act as he had not intended. He says: "I am not as yet, in the main, at all disappointed. I have been a good deal disappointed as it regards myself in not keeping up to my own plans; but now I feel entirely reconciled to that even; for God's plan was infinitely better, no doubt, or I should have kept my own. Had Samson kept to his determination of not telling Delilah wherein his great strength lay, he would probably have never overturned the house. I did not tell Delilah; but I was induced to act very contrary to my better judgment." God's plan was better than my own is the substance of the letter, and we doubt not that this rugged puritan, a lineal descendant in the direct line of Peter Brown of the "Mayflower," saw visions and dreamed dreams in his cell, and clearly perceived that the end of slavery in the United States was near at hand, and that his own death would hasten its downfall. He felt that *he*, as Samson by *telling* his secret was brought to the task of overturning the enemies' house, by *not keeping* his own plans had secured the destruction of slavery in the States. There can be no question now about his vision being correct. A few months later, the Twelfth Massachusetts marched out of Boston singing the John Brown song, and sang it in camp, and regiment after regiment caught up the air of it, and on the march and in the midst of battle descendants of the Puritans and of the Pilgrim Fathers, and other noble-hearted men, made fields and pathways resound with musical words of " John Brown's body lies a-mouldering in the grave," and of " his soul still marching on." The fore-seeing eye is yet in the world, and God's prophets have somewhat to do even in the nineteenth century.

He was a real Puritan, and, like the fathers from whom he descended, sternly religious. Baxter and Bunyan were the men with whom he sat and talked, through their books, and the bible was his chief adviser and guide. Selfishness had no place in his character, but generosity was the shining virtue of his life, and he was endowed with an exceedingly fine sense of justice. Fear he knew not; when told that the Missourians had marked him for death, he replied: "The Angel of the Lord will camp round about me." His destiny was linked with that of the slave; he felt that he *must* live and die for him; he was one of the instruments by which God worked out His will. In prison, he wrote: "I never did intend murder, or treason, or the destruction of property, or to excite or incite slaves to rebellion, or to make insurrection. The design on my part was to free the slaves."

Virginia and all the Southern States, though the great slave-owners called him a madman, were thrown into confusion by this Puritan and his nineteen men, and the baser sort would gladly have lynched him. They had for years taunted the antislavery party with cowardice, saying that they dared not preach emancipation in the South. In their imagined safely established power they sneered at the party of humanity, *were* sneering on that historic seventeenth of October, when, to their infinite surprise, momentary dread, and long-continued suspicion of a vast conspiracy against them, a few brave men stood up in their midst sword in hand to bear testimony with their lives against the crime of slavery. Never did lightning from heaven smite the human heart with terror more suddenly than

did this John Brown into the souls of men who
owned flesh and blood. They must find out who
had supported him, and see what power was behind him. Therefore, Senator Mason hastened to
Harper's ferry, and, finding the old puritan lying
on the floor of the armoury office, his face, hands
and clothes stained with blood which flowed from
his undressed wounds, proceeded to question him.
When was the organization formed? Who provided the money? Where did he get the arms?
Said Brown: " I will answer freely and faithfully
about what concerns myself — I will answer anything I can with honour, but not about others."
Asked: " How do you justify your acts?" he
answered : " I think, my friend, you are guilty of
a great wrong against God and humanity — I say
it without wishing to be offensive — and it would
be perfectly right for anyone to interfere with you
so far as to free those you willingly and wickedly
hold in bondage. . . . I think I did right, and that
others will do right who interfere with you at any
time and all times. I hold that the golden rule,
' Do unto others as ye would that they should do
unto you,' applies to all who would help others to
gain their liberty." . . . " I want you to understand, gentlemen," he said, " that I respect the
rights of the poorest and weakest of coloured people
oppressed by the slave system just as much as I

do those of the most wealthy and powerful. That
is the idea that has moved me, and that alone.
We expected no reward except the satisfaction of
endeavouring to do for those in distress and greatly
oppressed as we would be done by. The cry of
distress of the oppressed is my reason and the only
thing that prompted me to come here. . . . I wish
to say, furthermore, that you had better, all you
people of the South, prepare yourselves for a settlement of this question, that must come up for settlement sooner than you are prepared for it. . . . You
may dispose of me very easily. I am nearly disposed of now ; but this question is still to be settled
— this Negro question I mean ; the end of that is
not yet.'' Prophetic words, let the reader observe,
spoken by one whose soul was full of light, who in
a few days would join the '' Sons of the morning.''

Of course, the flesh jobbers called him a fanatic,
a fool, a madman, and his friends scarcely knew at
first what to say ; but in a little while they heard
God's message which came to them through his
death. Jefferson Davis called it : '' The invasion
of a state by a murderous gang of abolitionists, to
incite slaves to murder helpless women and children
. . . and for which the leader has suffered a felon's
death.'' Mr. Douglass said he was '' a notorious
man who had recently suffered death for his crimes
upon the gallows.'' Yes ; he was such an one to

the slave party. Slave-owners were as incapable of understanding a John Brown as the slave was of expounding Euclid ; they could not comprehend the man who said, while waiting for execution : "It is a religious movement ; — I regard myself an instrument in the hands of providence." He was a puritan ; they were slave-owners ; there was nothing in common between them. They were accustomed to the sight of the plantation, which debased them ; he, mostly with the pictures which bible stories inspired within him. Had he not read of Joshua taking a walled city by the blowing of trumpets and the shouting of his people ! And had he not studied the story of Gideon, who, with three hundred men, bearing only trumpets and lamps and pitchers, put to flight with mighty confusion the Midianites and Amalekites, who were like grasshoppers for multitude ! He would take *his* nineteen men against the slave power, and let God decide. *God did decide.* John Brown was hanged, and went to heaven ; and the influence of his life and death inspired the hearts of Northern men with feelings they never had before, and moved them to *look* more earnestly at the monster in front of them, and caused thousands of them to realize that more men would have to die, to *give their* lives to free the land from the great abomination. God did decide, from whose decision neither North nor South could escape.

Governor Wise, who went to see Brown, said in a public speech at Richmond : "They are mistaken who take Brown to be a madman. He is a bundle of the best nerves I ever saw, cut and thrust, and bleeding and in bonds. He is a man of clear head, of courage, fortitude . . . and he inspired me with great trust in his integrity, as a man of truth. He is a fanatic, vain and garrulous, but firm and truthful and intelligent." Not a bad opinion for the governor of the mother state of slavery to give of Brown, of which Emerson took note, and observed thereon : "Governor Wise, in the record of his interviews with his prisoner, appeared to great advantage. If Governor Wise is a superior man, or inasmuch as he is a superior man, he distinguishes John Brown. As they confer, they understand each other swiftly ; each respects the other. If opportunity allowed, they would prefer each other's society and desert their former companions." Whether Emerson's estimate of these two men be right or wrong we do not know ; but we do know that a lawyer, by name, Abraham Lincoln, was thinking of the incident of Harper's ferry, and that he said at Cooper College, February 27, 1860: "John Brown's effort was peculiar. It was not a slave insurrection, it was an attempt by white men to get up a revolt among slaves, in which the slaves refused to participate. In fact, it was so absurd that

the slaves, with all their ignorance, saw plainly
enough it could not succeed. That affair in its
philosophy corresponds with the many attempts
related in history at the assassination of kings and
emperors. An enthusiast broods over the oppression of a people, until he fancies himself commissioned by heaven to liberate them. He ventures
the attempt, which ends in little else than his own
execution." Abraham Lincoln felt much more than
he said ; he was speaking as a statesman. But he
uttered the truth. John Brown *had* brooded over
the oppression of the Negro, and *did* venture the
attempt to liberate him, and *was* executed. And
he did more. He left the incompleted effort to be
completed by the same Abraham Lincoln, whose
life also was sacrificed in the interest of the holy
cause. Only a few months after speaking his
memorable words on John Brown he was elected
President of the United States, which event was
quickly followed by the War of Emancipation,
after which the assassin ended his life ; but not
before he had saved the nation and set the Negro
free.

When Lincoln was assassinated the whole Christian world heard the news with sorrow ; but there
were men, who lived in civilized society, that rejoiced, and said in their hearts, if not with their
lips : " The South is avenged," which words Wilkes

Booth shouted in Ford's Theatre after shooting the president. He was a martyr, whose death sealed and made secure the glorious work which had been done. His assassination was another proof of the most weird fact of history, that martyrdom is the price good men have paid for human progress. Jesus Christ gave His life to save all men from sin and the ruin of disobedience, and His disciples feared not to emulate His example. Filled with His spirit, from His day until now, to give a larger application to Lincoln's words, noble men have brooded over the sorrows of the human family, and feeling heaven's call have ventured to assuage them, and, like John Brown, passed into rest by violence.

John Brown had, we think, a consciousness for years that the victory would be made sure by his own death, and if we were attempting more than a brief review of the efforts he made much evidence might be produced in support of that view. A few of his own words must suffice. Writing to Mr. Sanborn, a short time before he made his attack on Harper's ferry, he said : " I have only had this one opportunity in a life of nearly sixty years, and could I be continued ten times as long again, I might not again have another equal opportunity. God has honoured but comparatively a very small part of mankind with any possible chance of such mighty and soul-satisfying rewards. . . . I expect nothing but to 'endure hardness;' but I expect to effect a mighty conquest, even though it be like the last victory of Samson.''   A little while before his execution he wrote to his brother: '' I am quite cheerful in view of my approaching end, being fully persuaded that I am worth inconceivably more to hang than for any other purpose.   I count it all joy.   ' I have fought the good fight,' and have, as I trust, ' finished my course.' ''   To his cousin he said: '' When I think how easily I might be left to spoil all I have done or suffered in the cause of freedom, I hardly dare wish another voyage, even if I had the opportunity.''   To his children he wrote: '' I feel just as content to die for God's eternal truth on the scaffold as in any other way,'' and he added : '' as I trust my life has not been thrown away, so I also humbly trust that my death will not be in vain. God can make it to be a thousand times more valuable to his own cause than all the miserable service (at best) that I have rendered it during my life.'' To a minister of religion, who had written him a letter of sympathy, he replied : '' I think I feel as happy as Paul did when he lay in prison.   He knew if they killed him, it would greatly advance the cause of Christ ; that was the reason he rejoiced so. On that same ground ' I do rejoice.'   Let them hang me ; I forgive them, and may God forgive them, for ' they know not what they do.'   I have no regret

for the transaction for which I am condemned. I
went against the laws of men, it is true, but
'whether it be right to obey God or men, judge
ye.'" His last words to his family were: "John
Brown writes to his children to abhor with undying
hatred that sum of all villianes — slavery."

These words make a mirror, in which we may see
this man, John Brown, and if we be capable of looking behind the flesh, we may behold his very spirit.
For generations other good men had *talked* about
the slave trade, had felt, too, unutterable things in
respect of it, — sorrow, shame, indignation; but the
slave-owner dared them preach their theories in the
South, and mocked their piety. If the men of the
North so much as whispered the word *compulsion*,
the men of the South shouted *independence*, separation from the North, two United States, a North
and a South. In the senate and in the assembly
the voice of the demon was all-powerful, and no
remedy by talk or resolution could be had. John
Brown saw, heard and studied it all; "brooded
over it," to use Lincoln's words; felt that *he* must
do *more* than talk. Samson went into the house of
the Philistines, and pulled it down, and perished;
he would go boldly into the enemies' camp, and,
"though it be like the last victory of Samson,"
would try to effect a mighty conquest. He went,
and met the fate that befell Samson. The slave-

owners hanged him, and said "he has died a felon's death."

No separation from the North now, you flesh and blood jobbers, that you may continue the infernal traffic; this man Brown has destroyed all your schemes; his blood has been sprinkled upon the sons of God. You have killed him, hanged him to death, it is true, and it is also true that the nation has watched you, and her best men and women have written in their diaries what they think of it. Louisa Alcott has written: "The execution of St. John the Just took place December second," and Longfellow has set down in his journal: "This will be a great day in our history; the date of a new revolution, quite as much needed as the old one. Even now, as I write, they are leading old John Brown to execution in Virginia for attempting to rescue slaves. This is sowing the wind to reap the whirlwind, which will come soon." You ought not to have hanged John Brown, you buyers and sellers of flesh and blood; it was a mistake you made, to which you were moved by the blind wickedness that was in you; you shall ere long go out to see, and feel, the whirlwind. It is dangerous work, hanging a saint of God, though his methods have been indiscreet; they who are wicked enough to do it may look out for God's judgment, which *you* shall on no account escape.

At last the real prophets were aroused, to whom the country *had* to listen. Speaking of John Brown, Emerson said : " I wish we might have health enough to know virtue when we see it, and not cry with the fools ' madman ' when a hero passes ; " and the audience responded with prolonged applause. Again he said : " That new saint, than whom none purer or more brave was ever led by love of man into conflict and death — the new saint awaiting his martyrdom, and who, if he shall suffer, will make the gallows glorious like the cross ;" and the audience broke into intense enthusiasm. Thoreau said : " Christ was crucified some eighteen hundred years ago ; this morning, perchance, Captain Brown was hung. These are the two ends of a chain which is not without its links. He is not old Brown any longer ; he is an angel of light." Victor Hugo wrote : " In killing Brown, the Southern States have committed a crime which will take its place among the calamities of history. He was an apostle and a hero. The gibbet has only increased his glory and made him a martyr." And Mrs. Stearns wrote these words in respect of her husband : " On the second of December, Mr. Stearns yearned for the solitude of his own soul, in communion of spirit, with the friend who, on that day, would ' make the gallows glorious like the cross ; ' and he left Dr. Howe and took the train for Niagra Falls. There, sitting alone beside the mighty rush of water, *he solemnly consecrated his remaining life, his fortune, and all that was most dear, to the cause in whose service John Brown had died.*'' To these words of the real prophets of that time the country listened, and great was the result.

It was wrong, no doubt, as men speak, to attempt by ambush, force and invasion to subvert slavery in Virginia ; it is always better to appeal to reason and judgment, and have the matter settled by ballot. Enlightened forms of government and the Christian religion equally shrink from violence and the use of arms ; but in the case of the Negro in America the Southrons would not listen to appeal, would scarcely discuss the question, and finally, on that and some other issues, declared themselves a separate nation. What was to be done? John Brown had recently been hanged, and Abraham Lincoln more recently elected president, and the Christian conscience of the North was roused and instructed. What was to be done? With the boom of Southern guns firing on Fort Sumter millions of eyes turned to Harper's Ferry, and millions of hearts felt — *that is what has to be done*, and sooner we emulate the example of John Brown the better for the nation and the future of mankind.

It was done ; once and forever. Harper's Ferry could not be forgotten. Once more in the history

COL. ROBERT G. SHAW AND HIS COLORED REGIMENT, THE 54TH MASSACHUSETTS.

of man the stern, awful righteousness of the Old
Testament was seen on earth. Once again mothers
sent their sons with prayer and benediction to the
awful battle-field, to the conflict that was not for
gold, neither for dominion. And while fathers and
sons fought side by side, and together sang the
stirring words of the John Brown song, mothers
and daughters stayed at home and prayed, which
prayers were heard in heaven. And strange things
were seen. On the very spot in Virginia where
John Brown was hanged, the Webster Regiment of
Massachusetts stood on the first day of March, 1862,
and sang to the music of a Methodist hymn —

"John Brown's body lies a-mouldering in the grave,
But his soul goes marching on."

And many wept, and deep emotions were stirred,
and the God of heaven looked down on the sons of
men, and saw the good and the evil.

He saw that many men of the North would not
fight to free the slaves ; that the president himself
did not understand ; that the army of the North did
not unanimously believe it was a war of emancipation. The God of heaven guided the president, and
helped him in due time clearly to see the issue, and
strengthened him to declare the Negro free. It was
to retain the institution of slavery the South fought,
as stated distinctly by Jefferson Davis ; it was, in the

first instance, to preserve the union and defeat the rebellious states the North fought. Fighting for the union, as the history of the war clearly proves, the armies of the North made no progress toward victory; but when emancipation was declared and the Negro himself was brought into the struggle, victory was assured, and did finally attend their banners. It was victory wrought by the hand of the Almighty, which all may see who are not blind.

One more word from John Brown, the last he wrote.

" Charlestown, Jefferson Co., Virginia,
29th March, 1859.

Mrs. GEORGE L. STEARNS,
BOSTON, MASS.

My dear Friend

No letter I have received since my imprisonment here, has given me more satisfaction, or comfort, than your's of the 8th inst. I am quite cheerful: and never more happy. Have only time to write you a word. May God forever reward you and all yours.

My love to all who love their neighbours. I have asked to be spared from having any mock, or hypocritical prayers made over me when I am publicly murdered; and that my only religious attendants be poor little, dirty, ragged, bareheaded and barefooted, Slave Boys : and Girls, led by some old gray-headed slave Mother.

Farewell.   Farewell.

Your Friend
JOHN BROWN."

LAST MOMENTS OF JOHN BROWN

This letter was written on a half sheet of paper and inserted into the pages of a book, which Mrs. Brown took from the prison with other books and papers to her home. After a lapse of two months she found it, and sent it on to Mrs. Stearns, who received it as from the spirit world. Thoughtful of his friends, ever trustful in God, a devoted servant of Jesus Christ, — this *humane* man lighted the torch whose shining fell on the darkness of the slave's life, and fired the first shot to set him free.

The authorized tragedy is at an end; the Negro is free to work out his own destiny and overcome the unauthorized opposition of his haters as best he can. It has cost many precious lives to set him free; it required the strength of the strongest and the faith of the holiest to break his fetters.

Passing over the history of the war, we proceed to inquire into the use he has thus far made of his freedom, and to see if he have requited the valour and love of the dead and the living, which they displayed and cherished in his behalf. We look now for evidences of manhood in him, and for tokens of that divinity which the bible and all true churches declare is the quality of the human soul.

THE NEGRO AND HIS MANY DISADVANTAGES
AND BURDENS.

CHAPTER VI.

On the thirteenth of September, 1862, the Protestant Denominations of Chicago sent a deputation of gentlemen to President Lincoln to urge him to adopt measures that would quickly bring about the emancipation of the slave, and to advance the opinion that prompt action in the direction indicated was the only way to save the union. He listened to all they had to say with his usual patience and attention, and answered them in a characteristic speech. He said : " I do not want to issue a document that the whole world will see must necessarily be inoperative, like the Pope's Bull against the Comet. Would my word free the slaves, when I cannot even enforce the Constitution in the Rebel States? Is there a single court, or magistrate, or individual, that would be influenced by it there? . . . . . Now, then, tell me, if you please, what possible result of good would follow the issuing of such a proclamation as you desire? " The deputation urged in reply the good feeling of

Europe, which in their opinion would immediately be declared on the side of the union ; also arguments of humanity, and hinted that God might *then* be challenged to grant success to the union armies. President Lincoln replied : " I admit that slavery is at the root of the Rebellion, or at least its *sine qua non*. The ambition of politicians may have instigated them to act ; they would have been impotent without slavery as their instrument. . . . . Let me say one thing more : I think you should admit that we already have an important principle to rally and unite the people, in the fact that Constitutional government is at stake. This is a fundamental idea, going down about as deep as anything."

From the President it appeared not much might be expected. Some said he was a coward, others thought him lacking in sympathy for the slave, and even a few of his friends were afraid that he had no disposition to act as the anti-slave party desired and requested him. They were all wrong. Upon him rested a responsibility greater than any ever borne by President of the United States, *not* excepting Washington, and he knew it, and allowed neither individual nor society to hurry him out of *his* path of duty. He knew the power of the slave party, and the spirit of the slave system, and all through the long struggle waited for the guidance of God.

The lawlessness and barbarism of slavery, its

injustice and cruelty, its opposition to freedom of
thought, its degrading influence upon society, and
its repression of free speech even in the house of
prayer, were particularly manifest in the time of
Lincoln, who, from his watch-tower, saw much,
though not all, of the horrible work that was being
done. No pen will ever write, because it can never
be known, a full account of the life of the States
from 1860 to 1865. We can not even *imagine* the
state of Southern society at that time. The South
was controlled most pitilessly by a merciless cruelty
which stopped at nothing. Self-constituted courts
of law in the form of vigilance committees *made* law
as it was required for the punishment of offenders,
and executed their verdicts quite independently of
the Statutes of the Constitution. It was a condition
of national life which may be illustrated, but never
comprehended in all its vastness of evil.

Some time in the year 1860 the Rev. Solomon
McKinney went to Texas from Kentucky. He
believed in slavery, and taught that the bible sanc-
tioned it, and by *request* delivered a sermon on
"The relative duties of master and slave." The
sermon was "mild enough," as was to be expected
from a minister who believed that God approved
slavery ; but in it were many things which no
Christian could avoid saying on such a subject.
"*Relative* duties of master and slave" suggested

some thoughts to the mind of even Rev. Solomon
McKinney, to be spoken to both master and slave.
Much to his surprise, a public meeting was called
for the purpose of discussing his statements; and,
this reverend believer in slavery, who had preached
his sermon by *request* in Dallas County, Texas,
"was warned not to preach there again." Well,
he did not preach there again, but with another
preacher left Dallas County quickly as possible.
But it seems the public meeting which warned him
not to preach again in those parts meant somewhat
more than appeared on the face of the resolution
that was passed, and a party pursued the two
preachers, caught and brought them back, and
imprisoned them. Then armed men took them
from the jail, gave them eighty lashes each with
raw hide whips, until their "backs were one mass
of clotted blood and bruised and mangled flesh."
Such an event could not happen in any state or
country not demoralized by sin; but the depth of
the demoralization of the slave states may be dimly
perceived in it, and in what followed. Mr. Blunt,
Mr. McKinney's brother preacher, sent a memorial
to the Wisconsin legislature, in which he declared
he had never preached against slavery, and that
"for more than thirty years he had uniformly
supported the Democratic party in both state and
nation, and had sustained the views of that party

upon the issues between North and South.'' His
memorial, from our point of view, reflects disastrously upon himself, and suggests that he knew
little of the spirit of St. Paul, not to mention the
Christ, and it exposes the fiendish intolerance of
the slave states, and makes manifest the determination which obtained not to allow ''the other side
living room.''

It mattered not what a man's position was ; he
must conform to the opinion of the majority, which
was the slave party, or ''take the consequences.''
Many *did* ''take the consequences,'' and obeyed
conscience ; and, some fell into trouble quite innocently. A stone-cutter, an Irishman, when at work
on the South Carolina State House, remarked to a
fellow-worker that '' slavery caused a white labourer
at the South to be looked upon as an inferior and
degraded man.'' He ought not to have made that
remark, though true as anything that was ever said.
He was not prudent enough with his tongue in that
state of South Carolina ; it would have paid him to
remember that persons who told the truth were
punished there sometimes most severely. For making that simple remark he was thrust into jail, subsequently dragged through the streets, tarred and
feathered, and banished from the state after suffering
a week's imprisonment at Charleston.

President Lincoln, we have said, knew the power

of the slave party, and the spirit of the slave system, and that the evil could not be cast out so easily as the Chicago deputation thought. Reports of the injustice which was done, and of the cruelties that were perpetrated reached him every day, and his noble patience was tried to the utmost. He was under the most solemn oath, which every president of the States takes on inauguration, to keep intact the union and administer law justly and with impartiality ; yet was compelled to look upon the Southern States in rebellion, and upon the abrogation of statute law in hundreds of places, and for a time was unable to keep the oath he had taken. Ministers of religion, who ventured *not* to *denounce* slavery, but to make the mildest remarks in respect of slave masters' duties to slaves, were whipped almost to death, and artisans were tarred and feathered and banished for making casual truthful remarks. If such treatment in those cruel days was meted out to innocently offending *white* men, who can describe the tortures that were inflicted on *black* men? Mrs. Harriet Beecher Stowe, it was said, exaggerated in her wonderful book " Uncle Tom's Cabin ;" but no statement of the Negro's condition and sorrow has been nearer the truth. Her name. is embalmed in the history of the States, and enshrined in the hearts of all who love mercy and truth, and is an abiding inspiration of love to the

Negro ; and *we* shall ever be grateful to God for the interest which she and her illustrious brother Henry Ward Beecher took in us, and for the help they gave in the time of our struggle to gain education and usefulness.

The war continued. Contrary to expectation, it appeared farther from coming to an end than when it began. Discussions on the slave question were held in the senate, but no satisfactory conclusion could be reached. Europe looked on in silence, and with-held sympathy from the North, because no declaration was made against the hideous traffic in flesh and blood. Deputations waited on the president, and urged immediate proclamation of emancipation, but could not move him. He lived in the White House, a man of heart, conscience and benevolence, feeling keenly the terrible responsibility which Providence had thrust upon him. He was a great man, one of the greatest this world has seen, who desired above all things to do right. His wish always to do right was his reason for not declaring emancipation sooner than he did ; he waited for the opportune moment, and God revealed it to him.

The South had command of the slaves, and it is computed that not less than one hundred thousand of them were made to dig trenches and throw up embankments, which liberated so many white men to handle the rifle and take part in battles. The armies of the North had no such assistance, neither could they gain the mastery. The president's mind had solved the problem. He saw that the union was not to be saved if slavery were retained, and the proclamation of emancipation was written and carried in his pocket; yet he waited for the opportune moment. It came. The armies of the North gained a victory at Antietam, which was most welcome, and inspired every citizen of the North with hope and good feeling, and made a great impression on the continent of Europe. The Negro had been in bondage two hundred and fifty years: been the white man's beast of burthen; felt the whip, worn the chains and endured the agonies of oppression; wept as one without hope at the auctioneer's block when wife and child were sold away from him; prayed to a God he had heard of for deliverance or death; and, at last his day had come. The man of heart, and conscience, and benevolence, who lived in the White House; the great president who, with fortitude of mind never surpassed, had waited for the opportune moment; who said before he was inaugurated that he "would do whatever God wished him to do," now saw and understood the divine will, and made the following proclamation, which was flashed all over the continent: —

Whereas, On the Twenty-Second day of September, in the year of our Lord One Thousand Eight Hundred and Sixty-two, a Proclamation was issued by the President of the United States, containing, among other things, the following, to wit:

"That on the First day of January, in the year of our Lord One Thousand Eight Hundred and Sixty-Three, all persons held as Slaves within any State, or designated part of a State, the people whereof shall then be in rebellion against the United States, shall be then, thenceforth, and **FOREVER FREE**, and the *Executive Government of the United States*, including the Military and Naval Authorities thereof, *will recognize and maintain the freedom of such persons*, and will do no act or acts to repress such persons, or any of them, in any efforts they may make for their actual freedom.

"That the Executive will, on the First day of January aforesaid, by proclamation, designate the States and parts of States, if any, in which the people thereof respectively shall then be in rebellion against the United States, and the fact that any State, or the people thereof, shall on that day be in good faith represented in the Congress of the United States by members chosen thereto at elections wherein a majority of the qualified voters of such State shall have participated, shall, in the absence of strong countervailing testimony, be deemed conclusive evidence that such State and the people thereof are not then in rebellion against the United States."

Now, therefore, I, ABRAHAM LINCOLN, PRESIDENT OF THE UNITED STATES, by virtue of the power in me vested as COMMANDER-IN-CHIEF OF THE ARMY AND NAVY OF THE UNITED STATES in time of actual armed rebellion

94

against the authority and government of the United States, and as a fit and necessary war measure for suppressing said rebellion, do, on this First day of January, in the year of our Lord One Thousand Eight Hundred and Sixty-Three, and in accordance with my purpose so to do, publicly proclaim for the full period of one hundred days from the day of the first above-mentioned order, and designate, as the States and parts of States wherein the people thereof respectively are this day in rebellion against the United States, the following, to wit: — **Arkansas, Texas, Louisiana,** (except the Parishes of St. Bernard, Plaquemines, Jefferson, St. John, St. Charles, St. James, Ascension, Assumption, Terre Bonne, La Fourche, St. Mary, St. Martin, and Orleans, including the City of Orleans,) **Mississippi, Alabama, Florida, Georgia, South Carolina, North Carolina, and Virginia,** (except the forty-eight counties designated as West Virginia, and also the counties of Berkeley, Accomac, Northampton, Elizabeth City, York, Princess Ann, and Norfolk, including the cities of Norfolk and Portsmouth,) and which excepted parts are for the present left precisely as if this Proclamation were not issued.

And by virtue of the power and for the purpose aforesaid, I do order and declare that **ALL PERSONS HELD AS SLAVES** within said designated States and parts of States ARE, AND HENCEFORWARD **SHALL BE FREE!** and that the Executive Government of the United States, including the Military and Naval Authorities thereof, will recognize and maintain the freedom of said persons.

And I hereby enjoin upon the people so declared to be free to abstain from all

95

violence, UNLESS IN NECESSARY SELF-DEFENCE; and I recommend to them that in all cases, when allowed, they LABOR FAITHFULLY FOR REASONABLE WAGES.

And I further declare and make known that such persons of suitable condition will be received into the armed service of the United States, to garrison forts, positions, stations, and other places, and to man vessels of all sorts in said service.

And upon this act, sincerely believed to be AN ACT OF JUSTICE, warranted by the Constitution, upon military necessity, I invoke the considerate judgment of mankind and the gracious favor of ALMIGHTY GOD!

In Testimony Whereof, I have hereunto set my name, and caused the seal of the United States to be affixed.

[L. S.] Done at the CITY OF WASHINGTON, this First day of January, in the Year of our Lord One Thousand Eight Hundred and Sixty-Three, and of the Independence of the United States the Eighty-Seventh.

By the President,

A. Lincoln.

William H. Seward

Secretary of State.

This proclamation was made on the twenty-second
day of September, 1862, but the war continued until
1865. Its immediate effects completely answered
the expectations of the anti-slavery party, but in-
tensified the bitterness of the slave party. The
cause of the North, in the sympathy of christendom
and foreign nations, was immensely strengthened,
and righteousness was added to it, and for the first
time since Southern soldiers fired on Fort Sumter,
Christian communities and all good Americans, who
deplored and opposed the slave system, found themselves free to implore the blessing of the Almighty
on the armies of the North, inasmuch as *humanity*
and not *dominion* was now the defined cause. But
opposition to emancipation was declared by some
citizens of the North as well as by men of the
South, and even in the president's own state, mass
meetings were held against it. With him, however,
was no faltering. His absolute proclamation was
issued at the close of the hundred days of grace,
and in a letter to the people of his own state he
said it could not be retracted "any more than the
dead can be restored to life." In that same letter,
replying to their avowed determination not to fight
for the Negro, he said : "Some of them seem willing to fight for you." . . . "If they stake their
lives for us, they must be prompted by the strongest motive, even the promise of freedom, and the

promise being made must be kept." And he said, after expressing the hope of early peace, in rebuke of their bad spirit : "And there will be some black men who can remember that with silent tongue and clenched teeth, and steady eye and well-poised bayonet, they have helped mankind on to this great consummation, while, I fear, there will be some white ones unable to forget that with malignant heart and deceitful speech they have striven to hinder it."

From 1862, the year of emancipation, to 1865, the year of the close of the war, the condition of the Negro was not materially changed, his freedom notwithstanding. The war demanded, and received, almost all the thought and energy of the North. But tens of thousands of coloured men escaped from South to North, and were ultimately engaged as soldiers "at a salary of $10 per month, with $3 deducted for clothing — leaving them only $7 per month as their actual pay. White soldiers received $13 per month and clothing." Of the difference between his salary and that of the white soldier the Negro took no notice ; he was fighting for the good president who had declared him free, and for the final overthrow of the slave party, and to make safe his own liberty. Little did he expect, indeed he was unable to imagine, the conditions of life which were to be his after the good president's

assassination and the surrender of the Southern
army, which events happened within a few days of
each other. The story is a long and painful one,
and is probably the most disgraceful part of American history. It reveals the white man of the South
in the character of a demon, who was determined
to remand the freed coloured man as nearly as
possible to his former condition by state legislation. Alabama, Florida and Mississippi made it an
act of vagrancy, punishable with imprisonment, for
a *freedman* to leave the service of his employer
before the term prescribed in a written contact was
completed, which contract the Negro *had* in every
case to sign, or die of starvation on the public road.
Alabama, Florida, Mississippi, Texas and Louisiana made it a criminal offence for any person to
employ, feed or clothe a *freedman* who had left his
employer, under a penalty of a year in the house of
correction to both employer and employed, and five
dollars reward and ten cents a mile for travelling
expenses were paid to any officer of any state who
should take such an one back to his master. Florida
made it a criminal offence for any black man to enter
a white man's place of worship or public meeting,
or the white man's railroad car, under a penalty of
standing in the pillory for one hour, or be whipped
thirty-nine stripes, or *both* as the jury might decide.
South Carolina, Florida and Mississippi made it an

offence to keep any fire-arms, dirk, sword, ammunition or bowie-knife without a license, *which was under no circumstances granted to a Negro*, under a penalty of stripes and the pillory. President Lincoln had set the Negro free, but the Southern States, — immediately after peace was declared, and they had been restored to the union, exercising their state powers — made him sign contracts of service, forbade him to listen to a coloured preacher, punished him if he entered a white man's church, would not allow him to possess arms of any kind, and denied him "the right to acquire and dispose of property." Had President Lincoln not been murdered, it is safe to say that these iniquities would not have been permitted ; but President Johnson, himself once a slave-owner, who forfeited the confidence of his own party and the Christian world, suffered them without making one remonstrance, and in other ways helped make the *freed* Negro little different from a *slave*.

At the beginning of this chapter we saw what was done by the slave party, immediately *before* emancipation, to the Negro, and to white people who sympathized with him ; we are now seeing what was done immediately *after* emancipation. We can only give illustrations of horrid deeds and samples of inhuman enactments, which were done and made to create fear in the hearts of persons disposed to help the black man, and render it impossible for him to make progress. For several years a reign of terror existed, and in a short time several thousand murders were committed, and plunder and slaughter were effected the like of which has not been seen in any civilized country. It was stated in the senate that the following outrages and murders had been done. In Mississippi, twenty-three murders and seventy-six cases of outrage. In Alabama, two hundred and fifty murders, and one hundred and sixteen outrages. In Florida, one hundred and fifty-three cases of murder. In Louisiana in one year there were over one thousand murders. Who committed all these crimes? A society called the Ku Klux Klan, sometimes, The Pale Faces, and, Knights of the White Camelia, which was formed for the purpose of punishing Northern men and putting the "Nigger" in his proper place. Who the fiends were was never known, or never officially known, because witnesses dared not tell what they knew; to tell was to sign their own death warrant. Descriptions of a few outrages will illustrate the state of Southern life and of the Negro at that time.

In Eutaw, Alabama, a Negro named Sam Colvin was killed, and the prosecuting attorney, having worked up the evidence, announced that he would proceed against his murderers; but one day armed

men rode up to his hotel, forced the clerk to conduct
them to his room, shot him through the head, and
left him dying on the floor. The white attorney
must be silenced, and all white lawyers must be reminded that when Negroes were murdered nothing
must be done. "Governor Parsons said he had
never known of a conviction for the murder of a
Negro."

In Louisiana, Elias Hill, a poor Negro, who
could do no work, being a cripple from his youth,
lived as best he could. Most of his time was spent
in his cabin, where he sat day after day thinking
his own thoughts and knowing his own sorrow.
Being endowed with a strong intellect he could not
resign himself to eternal ignorance, and set about
gathering information in a novel manner. He
called the school children into his cabin as they
passed from school, and had them repeat to him
the lessons of the day, which he quickly learned.
Week by week he received instruction in this way
from his young teachers, and attained knowledge
of reading and writing, and became a school-teacher
and Baptist lay preacher. After emancipation he
thought himself free to teach and preach according
to his conscience, but forgot the society of the
White Faces. One day they visited him, and
charged him with various offences, of which he
was innocent. This poor man, who could not walk,

and never worked, failed to move compassion in them. They stripped him, horsewhipped his bare back, pulled his poor limbs apart, burned his few books and papers, and left him to get back to his cabin as best he might, or perish in the cold.

At the village of Cross Plains, Calhoun County, four coloured men and a white school-master were put to death by hanging and shooting. They were in charge of the officers of the law at the time, but very little evidence was forthcoming against them ; in fact no evidence could be produced, and it was certain they would be set at liberty. The White Faces, however, had decided they should die, and proceeded forcibly to take them from the authorities, and murdered them. This case was investigated, and nine persons were arrested, but the grand jury refused to indict a single one of them.

Teachers of coloured children were warned to stop their schools, and were told that, if they should refuse, they would have to choose between shooting, hanging, or whipping to death. In Aberdeen, Monroe County, Mississippi, twenty-six schools were closed in a short time, and even the state superintendent of schools was beaten by armed men. They called upon him and said : '' Our rule is, first, warning ; second, whipping ; third, death.'' They left him in a state of unconsciousness, having said they would next time call for his life. Nothing was too wicked for this society, which embraced all the Southern States, to do, and nobody who had sympathized with the North or helped the Negro in his necessity was safe. During its existence thousands of murders were committed, and outrages beyond count were done. "The information obtained from General Forrest and others established conclusively the following facts: the existence of the order; its prevalence in all parts of the confederacy; that numerically it was very strong; that it was so secret that its prescript or constitution was handed from member to member, so that the receiver knew not whence it came, but each reliable member sent it to some other reliable member whose fealty could be depended on; that it was composed of Southern citizens as distinguished from Carpetbaggers, or Northern men; that it worked by signs and not by oral or written orders; that crimes were committed in such a manner that the perpetrators were not usually known to each other." This diabolical society, which set itself to intimidate every friend of the Negro, reduce him to fear and dread, and continue the conditions of the slave time in an illegal manner, was certainly composed of the influential classes of the South and, it is believed, of the majority of Southern white people.

The Israelites in Egypt were not more miserable than the Negro in the States at the time of which this chapter treats; they *had* a *Moses* to lead them forth to liberty and national life. The Negro had no Moses to guide and inspire him; he had to begin at the lowest point of human existence, and as best he might work himself out of it. President Lincoln emancipated him, but his old owners, who commenced the war, did not understand *how* he *could* be a *free* man, neither were they great enough to refrain from pouring their wrath upon him for their defeat. Before the war he was a thing, and they bought and sold him, and became rich; after the war they were poor, and needed his help to repair their broken fortunes, which they would have at little cost; let him keep it back if he could. On the first day of the session, December 4, 1865, Mr. Wilson said in the senate "the condition of the freedman is worse to-day than on the day General Lee surrendered to General Grant." We shall yet see that he *did* rise in manhood and above many of his troubles.

CARPENTER SHOP, ORANGE PARK, FLORIDA.
SUSTAINED BY AMERICAN MISSIONARY ASSOCIATION.

CHAPTER VII.

THE BEGINNING OF BETTER DAYS, AND OF PROGRESS.

Failing to keep the Negro in the bondage of slavery, the slave party of the South might have known, had they not been blinded and rendered incapable of knowing by cruelty and inhumanity, that this reign of terror and this Ku Klux Klan could not continue, and that, sooner or later, coloured men must at least be free to labour for whomsoever would employ them, and to work out their own salvation as best they might. Gradually, their opposition notwithstanding, the enactments of the reign of terror period were repealed, and the Negro found himself at liberty to listen to a coloured preacher, have his own school, build his own church, deposit money in a bank, own land, and be elected to state office; that is, he was free to have and do these things; but, having no resources, he found it more difficult to use to his advantage these new privileges than a bird finds the building of her nest.

At first, immediately after the war, he gave himself to pleasure as he understood it. For nearly two hundred and fifty years he had laboured in ignorance and sorrow, and had known scarcely anything of enjoyment, probably nothing other than that afforded by his own musical faculty and undying happiness of spirit; now he was free he would take a holiday, and see what pleasure meant. It was to thousands of the race the pleasure of death, for which calamity no one could be blamed, neither the white man nor the Negro. His nature was, and is, the very essence of fun and frolic, and, owing entirely to ignorance of what religion really required of him, he would join in singing and prayer of the noisiest character, talk excitedly of the Saviour and heaven, and immediately after worship steal a fat chicken and have a good supper, or fall into some other deplorable and damaging sin. In this hour of wild delight he made for the large cities, and paid the penalty. A plantation Negro could live in the country and be healthy, but cities were death to him; and, during the first years of liberty large numbers of coloured men died prematurely. By this abandonment to pleasure, and by its untoward results, the friends who for years had fought his battle were alarmed; but in a short time he settled down to steady labour and to the working out of his own salvation.

The Freedmen's Bureau, which was instituted by
Abraham Lincoln's government, was appointed to
supervise and manage all abandoned lands, and
control all freed men and refugees from rebel
states; through the Secretary of War to issue provisions, fuel and clothing to destitute freedmen
and refugees; and, by the commissioner, under
the direction of the president, to grant the use of
abandoned tracts of land to loyal freedmen and refugees. This Bureau was established in the opportune moment, and was of the utmost use to the four
millions of freed Negroes; indeed without it both they
and the country would have suffered in many ways.

In 1870, Mayor O. O. Howard, Commissioner of
the Bureau, five years after his appointment, presented his first report, which to this day retains the
interest that attached to it when issued. In five
years 4,239 schools were established, 9,307 teachers
employed, 247,333 pupils instructed; also 74 high
and normal schools, which had 8,147 students;
also 61 industrial schools, with 1,750 students. Of
these schools the emancipated slaves themselves
sustained 1,324, owned 592 school buildings, and
raised two hundred thousand dollars of the total
sum which was expended during the term of five
years. It was a magnificent report the commissioner presented, which reflected upon the Negro
most creditably.

If anything could have proved to Southern slave-owners that the man they had bought and sold as a thing was capable of attaining and enjoying intellectual, as well as physical, life, the splendid energy and magnificent results of those five years, which were put forth and accomplished by men and women from whose limbs shackles had only just been struck, would have convinced them, and the whole subsequent history of Negro life in the South would have been different. Had they recognized their defeat good-naturedly, made proper terms with their former slaves, helped the Federal government to grapple with the problem of emancipation, assisted heartily all school building and educational efforts, and accorded without contest and bloodshed the freed people to civic rights, this report would end here with tables of statistics, showing the growth and development of the Negro race. But they were not convinced; the majority of them retained, and yet retain, their old opinions, and despised the black man.

In the South there are two parties to-day; one resolved to help the Negro, the other to oppress him; which are continuations of the parties of thirty years ago. Says one party: " We may take this stand : The Negroes are ignorant, are mendacious, are lazy, are dishonest, are licentious, and are therefore utterly unworthy of social and politi-

cal equality.   Granted, and granted to the fullest
extent ; but the more degraded, the world will say,
the greater obligation resting upon us to rescue
them from their blighted and brutalized condition.
. . . . They are with us to remain and they are
citizens, and the world will make it its business to
see that they are not arbitrarily kept in their present condition.   We can no more defend our attitude
toward the Negro, than could the Algerian Cor-
sairs defend their attitude to the Christian world."
" How shall these alien races dwell in safety side
by side, each free and unhampered in the enjoyment
of life and liberty and in the pursuit of its happiness ?   They are the descendants of one father and
the redeemed children of one God, the citizens of one
nation, neighbours with common interests, and yet
are separated by the results of centuries of development, by inherited traditions, by the spirit of caste
and by the recollection of wrongs done and suffered.
How shall the rights of all be duly guarded ?   How
shall the lower race be lifted up to higher stages
of human development ?   I answer, by the personal
endeavours of individuals of the higher race.   How
and where shall we begin ?   I answer, by building
firm and stable the conviction that the Negro is
a man and a citizen ; that the conditions of our
life are all changed ; that old things are passed
away, and that the new things which are come to

us demand, with an authority which may not be gainsaid, the effort of mind and heart and hand for the uplifting of the Negro.'' This is the Christian party, which stands for progress in its truest sense. They know that ignorance in any man, be he black or white, is dangerous, and that it is charged with peril to public life when it abides in millions of men ; and, remembering the injunctions of the Saviour, they seek to help the untaught of every colour in their effort to gain knowledge. In the dead years they regretted the lawlessness of their beloved South, and do so to-day, and would, were it in their power, change the hearts of all those citizens who oppose them and persecute the Negro. It has been a hard, sorrowful time for this Christian party during the last fifty years; but they possess the promise of God, and will yet make it impossible for any outrage to be committed, such as made the past infamous and disgrace the present. In the spirit of the Saviour they protest against violence, declare the brotherhood of man, and preach salvation, and will surely have success.

The other party says : '' The white men of the South and the Negroes learned to live together in peace while the Negro was in slavery. They can continue to live together so long as the latter is content to remain in subjection, so long as he recognizes the white as the master race. Under no other conditions is he fit to live in a civilized country. . . . His proper place is that of the white man's servant in a white man's country. The white man and the Negro cannot live together in peace under existing conditions. The white man must rule, the Negro must submit. This is a white man's country, a white man's government, a white man's civilization." "A little education is all the Negro needs. The excess has proved his ruin. Let him learn the rudiments, to read and to write and to cipher, and be made to mix that knowledge with some useful labour. Too much education and too little work are the prime cause of the growing antipathy. With the whites there are some reasons for a higher education, for the professions and the trades are open to them, but all these are closed to the Negro." "An attempt to develop the Negro skull into that of the Caucasian is just as idle, not to say absurd and wicked, as would be the educating of apes, with a view of developing their skull with those of human beings. All attempts to force upon them the education and civilization of the white man are not only unphilosophic but absurd and detrimental. In a zoological sense they belong to the genus homo, but the mode of their creation concludes them only in the highest order of animals, and subjects them to the dominion of the Adamite." This is the anti-Negro, anti-Christian, party, which stands for oppression and retrogression. Dominion, supremacy and authority for the white man are their watch-words. The Negro is not fit to live in civilized society ; he must submit to the white man ; God has ordained it that he labour under the white man's rule ; "a little education is all the Negro needs." Can the reader realize that these awful statements are being made to-day? It is almost nineteen hundred years since Jesus Christ lived among men, and revealed the fatherhood of God and taught the brotherhood of men, and in all the years servants of His have preached His gospel ; yet here are men in the South of the United States who refuse even to be human in conduct, who persecute and lynch to death a brother-man. To-day, let this be remembered, they will not allow a coloured man to enter their churches, nor permit him to ride in the same railroad car with them, and in some States of the South a white man and a coloured woman can not marry. Hotels are closed against coloured men of every station in life ; proprietors dare not admit them. Even at the last republican convention, held at St. Louis, which nominated Mr. McKinley for the presidency, at which many coloured men attended as delegates, there was serious trouble about lodging them. In fact they had no lodging for a time, and at last special provision had to be made for them. Of this disgraceful episode one paper remarked, "foxes have holes, and birds of the air have nests, but coloured delegates have not a lodging." It is difficult to write calmly of such a state of society, and would be impossible if the Christian party did not exist. It is the old sin of the past, inherited by a generation of men not wise enough to see its wickedness. But their opposition is doomed to fail even as their fathers' effort to retain slavery failed; their unholy determination not to admit the Negro into civilization notwithstanding, the beginning of better days is here and progress is being made. Right must prevail; God's will shall be done; righteousness will fill the earth as the waters cover the sea; this anti-Christian party is doomed to final defeat.

Yes; better days have begun and progress is being made, which the following statistics abundantly prove. They are the statistics of 1890, which we give as those of 1896, that any exaggeration may be discounted. In the matter of wealth the Negro has made great progress, and not a little in the professions and literature. Let the figures tell the tale. First, his wealth in business and property.

> In New York . . $17,400,756
> Louisiana . . . 18,100,528
> South Carolina . 12,500,000
> Pennsylvania . 15,300,648

Texas	18,010,545
Mississippi . .	13,400,213
Georgia . . .	10,415,330
North Carolina .	11,010,652
Alabama . . .	9,200,125
Florida	7,900,040
Massachusetts .	9,004,122

and in the other states proportionately. It is computed that two hundred and sixty-three million dollars worth of property is held to-day in the United States by the Negro race. How dare the anti-Christian party say that all Negroes are lazy? Lazy people do not accumulate wealth. Many Negroes are no doubt lazy, but in the way it is put it is a falsehood told to answer a base purpose. But it is true that this race which to-day possesses so much property owned not one cent thirty years ago. Then, Negro men and women toiled for the white man, for which they received food, not much clothing, and no education. The world cannot but admit that great energy must have been exercised for so much to be accomplished in so short a time.

We find the Negro has invented many things of utility, and give the names of a few of them as proof of mental development.

A Corn-stalk Harvester, Wm. Murray, Virginia.

A Locomotive Smoke-stack, L. Bell, Washington.

A Fire Extinguisher, T. J. Martin, Michigan.

A Cotton Cultivator, E. H. Sutton, N. Carolina.
A Joiner's Clamp, D. A. Fisher, Jr., Washington.
A Rotary Engine, B. H. Taylor, Mississippi.
Apparatus for Transmission of Messages by Electricity, G. T. Woods, Ohio, and scores of other inventions. Mr. Woods' invention was assigned to the American Bell Telephone Company, Boston. The anti-Negro party say he must learn the rudiments of education, to read, cipher, and write, and then do manual labour. It is true that the majority of all races of men must do manual labour, and find good therein, also the will of God ; but it is a denial of divine providence to say the Negro can not enter higher fields of human effort. His inventions prove him intelligent, as his accumulated property establishes his industry.

In literature he has done more than enough to claim a place among men devoted to letters. We do not say that the literary Negro can be ranked with men of the most brilliant attainments, neither do we think it ; but when we find the schools of Ohio using a Greek Grammar for beginners, written by W. S. Scarborough, a coloured man, of Wilberforce, Ohio, we can and do say that the natural incapacity theory is destroyed. Since 1865 over one hundred books have been written by Negroes, not a few of which may be found in American Public Libraries. Even London received Phillis Wheat-

ley, a young black girl, of Boston, and was astonished by her sweet poetry, in or about 1792. This
Phillis Wheatley, whose history is most interesting,
of whom we shall take notice in another chapter,
was an imported slave, and she was deeply beloved
by her master, John Wheatley, and by his wife.
So pure and simple and refined were the poems she
wrote, that many white men doubted their authorship ; but her master and certain ministers of Boston
proved that she *was* the author. The mental incapacity theory is doomed, and the men who preach
it are certain of confusion. If the Negro were little
better than an ape, as many have asserted, he would
not write Greek Grammars, articles for Harper's,
The Atlantic Monthly, The North American Review,
and other papers and journals, neither would Negro
girls compose sweet and charming poetry. The
possibilities of a race of men are never gauged by
the work and conditions of its *lowest* members, but
by those of its *highest* members, which is a just
method, and all we ask is that it be applied to the
Negro race. The result will be satisfactory.

In the public schools of the United States 23,866
Negro teachers are employed, and there are 1,460,000
pupils receiving education in the free schools. In
the medical profession not less than five hundred
properly graduated Negro doctors are at work, most
of whom are successful. In the pulpit thousands

of coloured preachers work successfully, many of whom have received two or three year's education, and some have graduated in the ordinary manner from theological institutions. In the realm of law about three hundred Negroes have, if not distinguished themselves, succeeded in winning a place, and do enjoy, varying in degree, extensive practice. One is a circuit court commissioner, several are judges, many are clerks of courts, and a few are city attorneys. The value of church property owned by Negroes is not less than $22,000,000, and church members number about 2,600,000. This is progress, we say, for which the Negro's friends ought to be thankful.

A few centuries ago the coloured man was a Pagan, knew nothing of righteousness, and in America was pushed into slavery. He came out a free man, left behind him forever the chains which once bound his wrists, and had a place accorded him in the national life of the States. He came out a free man, but was ignorant, had many gross faults, yet knew somewhat of God and of Jesus Christ. A higher life than his had touched him, which he did not understand, yet cherished it. It did not touch him in vain ; in his heart forthwith sprang up a great yearning for knowledge. The day on which the first school for freedmen was opened in September, 1861, under the auspices of

the American Missionary Society, at Hampton, Virginia, three hundred and fifty scholars were enrolled,
and in the evening of the same day three hundred
more were added. The numbers continued to increase until the enrollment of the day school was
1,200, and the night sessions gathered 800 more,

LAUNDRY, STRAIGHT UNIVERSITY.
SUSTAINED BY AMERICAN MISSIONARY ASSOCIATION.

making a total for this single school of 2,000 pupils
daily. Many of them were adults, who came after
the fatigue of a hard day's labour, that they might
gather the rudiments of knowledge. That was in
1861, and to-day there are 1,460 coloured children in
public schools. At Tougaloo University, also at
Tuskegee and Hampton Normal, industrial training

is a great feature of the course of education. Boys
are instructed in agriculture, horticulture, harness-
making, cabinet-making, wood-carving, printing,
typesetting, bookbinding, shoemaking, and other
trades, and girls in housekeeping, cooking, laundry-
work, dressmaking, millinery, nursing and hygiene,
all which reminds one of the saying of a Southern
educator : " The Negro is coming to have what the
white man wants, and this is sure to secure to him
his safety and his rights." From that day in 1861
until now a great struggle upward has been made,
and in presence of so many evidences of success it
is safe to say that better days are with us in which
progress is being surely made.

Writing in the name of the American Missionary
Association on " The Progress of the Negro," Rev.
Geo. W. Moore, of Tennessee, field missionary,
says : —

" Thirty years have wrought mighty changes for
the South, but the greatest wonder is the progress
of the Negro. The freedom of the Negro gave him
a new era, and opened doors of opportunity for his
material intellectual and spiritual advancement.
The distance between the slave and the freeman is
world-wide. His freedom has improved his condition and increased the wealth and prosperity of the
South. Thirty years is a short period in the life of
a race, and yet it is sufficient to note its progress.

The free Negro has been of greater advantage to the South, and has done more for its development than at any time during his slave life. This is so patent that we are safe in asserting that the prosperity of the South is largely dependent upon the elevation of the Negro. He comprises one-third of its population and is a large factor in its development and progress.

His material property enriches it to the degree of the increase. His skill as a laborer is to her advantage, for he is the laborer of the South. His education decreases the illiteracy and increases the intelligence of the South. His religious and moral advancement lifts from the South a weight of superstition and vice. The recognition of his manhood rights develops his selfhood and makes him a better man and a more loyal citizen. Elevate him and you lift up the South, degrade him and you pull down our fair land. The Negro has made rapid progress in spite of his limitations. He has come up from the depths of slavery, poverty, ignorance, superstition and degradation to a freedman, taxpayer, wage-earner, a degree of intelligence and a more enlightened view of Christianity and morality, and to be a citizen of a great country. The pen of Lincoln and the sword of Grant helped to make this possible, but the work of Christian education and an enlightened Christianity, which came to us by

Northern philanthropy, through the schools and churches of the American Missionary Association and kindred organizations, have done more for our uplifting and advancement than any other influence. The work of educating and uplifting the Negro is the brightest page in Southern history. This is indeed the silver lining of our dark cloud. The heroic men and noble women of this grander Army of the Republic, commissioned by the American Missionary Association, proclaimed liberty to the mind and soul as well as freedom to the body of the Negro. Some of them have served for nearly a quarter of a century in the work of the education, Christianization and uplifting of the Negro.

Before referring more fully to the educational advancement of the Negro let us briefly consider his material progress. Coming out of slavery with nothing and meeting with difficulties which have confronted him at every step of the way, his material progress has been remarkable. It is estimated that the Negro pays taxes on over two hundred and seventy-five million dollars' worth of property, besides personal property, churches, schools, etc.

They are entering into the real estate and insurance business. I could give numerous examples of colored men who are successfully conducting dye and steam cleaning works, drug stores, undertaking establishments, mercantile business and all kinds of

work.   The following is a partial list of employment
of Negroes in Nashville, Tenn. : teachers, ministers,
lawyers, physicians, dentists, merchants, all kinds
of mechanics, owners of livery stables, undertakers,
contractors, firemen, mail carriers, coachmen and
teamsters owning their own teams, laborers of all
kinds, etc.

But we are still a poor people and must. greatly
improve our condition materially.   In order that
the Negro may have better homes and improve his
condition materially he should receive better wages
for his labor.   He is the laborer of the South on
the farm, in the workshop, domestic life, and is
branching out into professional life.   He is the
most patient and untiring worker in the South.

What is to be done to better the Negro's condition
as a wage earner?   He cannot strike for higher
wages with safety.   The Negro can refuse to work
for low wages, but he has no redress or means of
appeal for higher wages only as the master-class
may choose to increase his pay.

The most hopeful sign of the progress of the
South is the education of the Negro.   What a field
of endeavor among the eight millions of our people.
It is estimated that twenty-five thousand Negro
teachers are teaching over a million and a half of
our children in the public schools of the South.
About fifteen thousand of these are trained teachers,

most of whom have been trained in the schools of the American Missionary Association. Over four million colored people have learned to read since the war. The schools of the American Missionary Association are training teachers and leaders for our people in the South. Our schools are well located and classified to meet the wants of the people ; some are in our large centers of population like Nashville, New Orleans and Charleston, and others are in country places like McIntosh, Ga., and Cotton Valley, Ala. At Fisk we have a college, normal department and departments of music, theology and industrial training. At Talladega and Tougaloo in the Black Belt of Alabama and Mississippi we have large farms and workshops in addition to the college and normal training ; useful industries are taught in all of our Association schools. . . . . .

The religious progress of the Negro has not been as rapid and as great as his material and educational progress. He brought with him from slavery an inheritance of superstition that has been hard to overcome ; then, too, the masses of the people have had ignorant and, in many cases, corrupt men as ministers. And yet there has been progress in his religious life, work and worship. This progress has been largely due to the stimulating effect of our Congregational churches in the South, and of the students who have gone out from our American

Missionary Association schools. This progress may be seen in the improved character of their churches and meeting-houses, better men of intelligence and piety as preachers, and improved methods of work. The great need of the colored people is evangelization, ingathering and uplifting. This we are doing in their behalf. We recognize the fact that we have duties to perform as well as rights to maintain; that we are to seize our opportunities rather than emphasize our grievances; yet the real progress of the Negro cannot be measured without considering his advancement in manhood and self-hood. Is his manhood respected, does he receive his rights before the law, is caste prejudice waning? What is his status as a man and a citizen? These are vital questions which affect his destiny.

Put a premium on character, right living and justice. Make it possible for me to say to my son: ' My boy, you are an American; love your country, honor her laws, fight her battles and preserve her free institutions. Be noble and true and good and have a character void of offense, and good people of every race and of every clime will love and respect you and give you every right to which your worth entitles you.' I would rather inspire my son with such sentiments than that he should hold the highest position in the land. It is our hope that some day we can truthfully set such a goal before every boy

and girl of every race in our broad land ; that the
white boys and girls of Florida and the black boys
and girls of South Carolina may alike have an
opportunity to rise."

Such testimony from one whose life is devoted to
the work of Christianity in " *Darkest America,*" as
he calls it, can scarcely be over-estimated, it is so
valuable ; but the reader must not think that perse-
cution is ended. The anti-Negro party is very
much alive and fiercely active. They do *not* respect
the Negro's manhood ; *refuse* to accord him equal
rights before the law ; *cherish* caste prejudice ; *will
not recognize* the progress which has been made.
In the Black Belt of the South, back on the plantations, conditions of life for thousands of Negroes
are little better than they were thirty years ago,
perhaps for many they are worse, and in hundreds
of Southern cities the coloured man — not to mention
coloured women, who are subjected to every kind
of insult — is under the utmost obligation to " keep
his place " or take the consequences. Occasionally
he forgets to keep what is called his place, and
forthwith suffers for it ; and sometimes mad crowds
seize him for no offence, neither real nor imagined,
and ill-treat him, and often hang perfectly innocent
men and riddle their bodies with shot. However,
better days are with the Negro, and will continue
with him. It is a pleasure to find so much of good

among so much that is bad, and though lynchings yet are done, the story of which will be told in another chapter, and though the anti-Negro party oppose every step forward and upward, the Negro's star of progress has risen, never more to set.

LYNCHING OF THE WAGGONER FAMILY IN TENNESSEE. 1893,
[FATHER, SON, SON IN LAW AND.DAUGHTER] FOR NO KNOWN
OFFENCE.

CHAPTER VIII.

LYNCHINGS.

Progress is never made by any man or any race of men by methods of ease; opposition must be overcome, pain can not be avoided, exhaustion is frequently realized, and despair often fills the heart. It is easier for a young man of good birth and sound education to make progress than for one born in ignorance and reared among debasing conditions. The latter finds himself at "the bottom of the ladder" with scarcely strength enough to place his foot on the first rung, and when he makes his initial effort he is more likely to be pushed back by the pressure of social influence than helped forward. Character is asked for when he applies for even the most menial position, and he has no character to give; but is desperately anxious to earn one. If they who control the markets of labour were more willing to take a little risk, and would extend confidence to this sort of man, and tell him so, this world would have fewer tramps and jails would be less frequently full.

It is impossible, however, in this connection, to forget political economy, supply and demand, the overstocked condition of labour markets, and the natural desire of employers to engage only the most trustworthy employees. Political economy is, no doubt, a correct science, and perhaps it is dangerous to depart from its practice. Supply and demand can not be forgotten ; a merchant may not employ more people than the proper discharge of his business requires. The overstocked labour market is a problem which remains to be solved ; *must be solved*, if social trouble on a vast scale is to be avoided. The multitude of men and women who must earn bread or starve, or live by sin, if it be not done by men of understanding, will one day try to solve the problem themselves, and will fail ; by which attempt and failure much will be destroyed that ought to be preserved, and society will know by experience somewhat of the agonies and losses of the French Revolution, which was a blind effort of the masses to reorganize the conditions of human life.

Thirty years ago the Negro was a man without character. Born in slavery, reared in debasing servitude, and kept in ignorance and poverty, he was the unconscious debaser of all who came in contact with him, always excepting those who laboured in the name of Christ to improve him. Nobody trusted him, the majority of the inhabitants of the South despised him, and they for whom he had laboured in the bad days of slavery would only employ him on their own terms, which circumstances compelled him to accept or die. To get *his* foot on the first rung of the ladder meant an effort which few are capable of imagining, and it is not surprising that so many of his race have so far failed ; but it is surprising that so many have done so well.

The progress described in the last chapter is that of *many* of the race, but not of the *whole* race ; in the "Black Belt of the South," the "Plantation South," millions of Negroes live in conditions little better, if not worse in some districts, than those of slavery times. But even here an awakening is manifest. These millions of human beings, all over thirty-five years old born in slavery, are asking for better preachers, for ministers "who can teach them something," which is a splendid token of good. The preachers they have been accustomed to hear are losing their influence. "We used to listen," said a Negro man at a recent meeting, "to those whooping and hollering preachers who snort so you could hear them over three hundred yards, and we would come home and say, 'that's the greatest sermon I ever heard.' But now we want men who can teach us something." "Our preachers are not what they ought to be," said one woman. "We have got too many gripsack preachers — men who go around from church to church with a grip-sack, not full of sermons, but of bottles of whiskey, which they sell to the members of their congregation." No better sign of heart and soul uplifting might be had ; when masses of men and women ask for a purer religion, they are not far from the Kingdom of God.

Now, it would be thought that the higher race, the white race, of the South would rejoice in these tokens of good, and, if only from selfish motives, hasten to render help in every possible manner. But the majority of the white South do not rejoice, neither are they willing to help the Negro upward ; they wish to keep him down. They say "we don't want the Negroes to get educated or to get rich, the more educated they are and the richer they are, the worse it is for us. It is a big stick in their hands." Visciousness could not go farther than this, and it were not easy to find denser ignorance of social economics even among plantation Negroes. The white men of the South do not yet know that having millions of ignorant men among them keeps back their own development in human and spiritual things.

This is the spirit which moves them to do the horrible deeds that will be described in this chapter, which perhaps the reader will find it difficult to believe, so terrible are they. But the truth must

be told. Outrages are being committed in the
South, chiefly upon the Negro, which are a disgrace to civilization, and are done to "keep him in
his place." He *was* a slave, and could be loaded
with chains, branded with hot irons, or whipped to
death, and now he is a free man, why should he be
treated differently? For centuries the whites of
the South had treated him so, had classed him with
hogs, and sold him as a thing; they could not feel
that he was a man, and were incapable of knowing
their own debasement; and, the majority of them
are yet unchanged. Proceeding at once to give the
fearful history of torture and murder, the reader
may believe that nothing is related that can not be
established by evidence, and that all is told to
advance the Negro's cause.

We must first give statistics, which are horrible
enough, and then a few details, which are more
horrible.

1882	. . .	52 Negroes were lynched.
1883	. . .	39 " " "
1884	. . .	56 " " "
1885	. . .	77 " " "
1886	. . .	73 " " "
1887	. . .	70 " " "
1888	. . .	72 " " "
1889	. . .	95 " " "
1890	. . .	100 " " "
1891	. . .	169 " " "

1892	. . .	160	Negroes	were	lynched.
1893	. . .	202	"	"	"
1894	. . .	190	"	"	"
1895	. . .	171	"	"	"
1896	. . .	131	"	"	"
1897	To date*	40	"	"	"

The United States must be called, if offence is to be avoided, a civilized country ; indeed, Americans call it a Christian Country. Churches and ministers of religion abound, and charity is dispensed on a large scale therein. Prayers are offered before God daily for every kind of imagined blessing and furtherance of the kingdom of heaven, and tens of thousands of *pious* men and women believe they do the will of the Almighty, who to them is " Our Father ; " yet parsons and saints are practically dumb in respect of this gigantic outrage and devilish wickedness. Some, who are only a few when compared with the millions of American *Christians*, protest most earnestly ; but let the citizens of the proud United States remember that murders are committed openly in their towns and cities, and that they are guilty of a shameful silence in respect of them

In fifteen years and three months 1,697 Negroes have been lynched in defiance of statute law and in the very presence of legal officials, which is a fact

---

*This number is not given as accurate, but is approximately correct.

so horrible that one is tempted to believe it is not to be surpassed, perhaps not equalled, in brutal wickedness even in *Darkest Africa*. President, Senators, Congressmen, Governors of States, and Mayors of Cities — each and all of them know that this diabolical work has been done, and is continued until now, and that the murderers go unpunished, but seem to be incapable of stopping it. Power and authority appear to be vested in nobody to command Governors of States to arrest and punish the fiends who so openly abrogate the Constitution, and, to tell plain truth, not many governors seem to take much notice of the murders which are done almost beneath the windows of their homes. Let but one governor be brave enough to arrest every person who shall take part in the next lynching in his state, and let them be sent to Washington for trial, — this for the simple reason that evidence would count as nothing in their own city — and let every one of them be hanged, and lynchings will cease. If power to do this be non-existent, it ought to be created ; if the authorities are unwilling to create it, we see not how they can escape the charge of a silent, guilty connivance, and of being possessed in some degree of the murderous spirit. It is futile to say that lynchers can not be arrested ; no sane man believes for a moment that sufficient force does not exist in the United States to coerce any city into

obedience, and compel any number of citizens to surrender known murderers and give evidence against
them.   The authority and needful power *do exist*,
and it were better for the moral life and right
development of the population of the States if they
who are appointed to use them had the courage and
righteousness to do so.   The country will one day
pay a great price for this national crime, if it be not
destroyed, as she paid in blood and treasure for the
sin of owning slaves.

Of these 1,697 lynchings only a few may be
described, and the most loathsome details shall not
be reproduced.   The record is foul and revolting
enough without added effects of language ; as bad
as anything in human history.

In the town of Jackson, Tennessee, in 1886, a
black woman was lynched because a white woman
who engaged her as cook had by *some one* been
poisoned.   It appears that a box of rat poison was
found in the cook's room, which was evidence
enough of her guilt in the eyes of the mob, and she
was soon lodged in jail.   Thence she was dragged,
stripped of every garment, and hanged perfectly
naked in the public court-house square, without
protest of any kind being made.   No trial was
held, neither was anyone arrested for the murder ;
the inhabitants, officials of the law included, looked
upon the matter quite complacently.   But what

followed? The husband of the poisoned woman became insane, gave every indication in his ravings of his own guilt, and *died* a *maniac*, leaving behind him at least a suspicion that *he* was the *poisoner* of his wife.

In the vicinity of Columbia, Matagorda, Texas, in September, 1887, a coloured constable named Massena was serving writs, which was his duty. A white man named Sanborn was among the number upon whom he had to serve a writ, and he called in the ordinary manner at Sanborn's house to discharge his legal task. The white man, using profane language, declared that no "nigger" should arrest him, and before Massena had time to do more than say he was only doing his duty, Samborn shot him, — and fled. What followed? His white friends gave out the report that Sanborn had been killed by the Negroes. Then an armed mob *and the sheriff* visited the coloured settlements on Sunday, arrested without warrant many negroes, killed five and wounded seven of them for refusiug to be arrested, and then gave an alarm of a *Negro rising against the Whites*. For some days it was the ordinary affair of daily life for " Niggers " to be forced to flee from the neighbourhood to save themselves, and numbers of them were shot without compunction. Of course, nobody was punished; but Sanborn was brought from his hiding place, regiments were marched through Matagorda, and a ball was held to wind up the affair. The Turks in Armenia have not done worse than this.

In the month of August, 1888, at New Iberia, Louisiana, ten Negroes were done to death for "being too prosperous, and not behaving correctly toward white people." Antonio Smith, Ramson Livingstone, Peter Simon, John Simon, Thomas Simon and Sam Kokee, all of them most respectable men and property owners, and four others whose names are not given, were butchered by a mob for no crime whatever. The authorities took no notice of the matter, and the murderers were thought nothing the worse for their "sport among the Niggers." It is a sport which will yet cost the states more than she imagines.

In the year 1889, and during all his life, a coloured doctor named Rosamore Carmier lived in Lafayette Parish, Louisiana, with his wife and daughter, and owned his home. The whites did not like "nigger doctors" to live among them, and told Carmier so, and ordered him to "get out" several times. Seeing he had no intention of "getting out" they whipped him most severely, and told him they would "make him go." He stayed where he was. One night the usual mob surrounded his house and demanded that the door be opened, which Carmier knew meant that he was to be lynched. He fired on the mob and fled. Then the mob broke in, destroyed his goods, dragged out his sixteen-year-old daughter, and cut her throat; and, one report says, "washed their hands in her blood." His wife quite unintentionally told them the way her husband had gone, whom they pursued and overtook and shot him. For being a doctor and living in a respectable manner with his wife and daughter, poor Carmier was ordered to go away, and because he refused he and his child were murdered.

In June, 1890, a Negro named George Swaysie, who lived in East Feliciana, was butchered by a "large company of white men." The police did not want him, because he had done no crime; but the mob thought it time for a "Nigger to be lynched," and therefore lynched him. The poor man was in bed when the white men arrived at his house, but they dragged him out into the rain and dark night, and "despatched him." What for? Until now nobody has been able to find out. It is enough for a company of white men to agree that a certain "Nigger" has lived long enough, or to imagine he is a nuisance to them, or to have a petty quarrel with him, and, decision being made, he is lynched, and all legal authorities look on in pitiable helplessness.

At Tullahoma, Tennesseee, Will Lewis, a Negro boy of eighteen years, was lynched in the month of

August, 1891. It is no part of the writer's duty to defend drunkenness, but every man must in justice demand that even drunkards receive fair trial and judgment. But when a boy of eighteen years — only eighteen — is taken and murdered in cold blood for being drunk and impertinent to white people, what can any one say? Thought is paralyzed, and speech is impossible; one can only look on the crime and wonder at the condition of the morals of the country in which it is done. Will Lewis may have been impertinent to white people, he may have been drunk, which charges were never proved; but compared with his white murderers, he was an angel.

At Hollendale, Mississippi, Lou Stevens was hanged from a railway bridge, because she was suspected of being accessory to the murder of a white man who regularly committed adultery with her. This happened in 1892, and in the same year a girl of fifteen years of age was in a similar manner hanged at Rayville, Louisiana, because the mob believed she had poisoned white persons.

At Texarkana, Texas, on the twentieth day of February, 1892, Edward Coy was burned to death. He was taken alive and tied to the stake, and in the presence of thousands of persons the white woman who charged him with assault applied the match.

In the same year, 1892, at Jonesville, Louisiana, a triple murder was committed by the mob on a father, son, and daughter. This Negro was suspected of murdering a white man. First, the inhuman inhabitants took his son, aged sixteen, and his daughter, aged fourteen, and hanged them, subsequently filling their bodies with bullets, and then lynched the poor father himself, who perhaps was not sorry to follow his children.

In Memphis, Tennessee, not less than thirty thousand coloured people make their home, and to the best of their ability help in the ordinary manner of citizens to make the town prosperous. Of these thirty thousand quite a number are poor, and not a few are often short of food, which is a condition that is the portion of many white people in any similar number of population. In July, 1892, a coloured man named Lee Walker was compelled by want to beg, and did unfortunately commit a small offence for which ordinary law would have punished him with a short imprisonment. He asked alms of two white women who were driving to Memphis, and was refused. Then he pulled one of the women from the buggy, and immediately ran away. He cannot be excused for doing even so small a violence on an unprotected woman ; his offence deserved and ought to have received legal punishment. But it was given out that a coloured man had attempted outrage upon a white woman, and forthwith a man-hunt was started by companies of passionate citi-

zens.   In the course of ten days Walker was caught
and taken to Memphis jail, where he ought to have
remained for decent trial and just sentence.   But
the mob took the law into its own hands, dragged
him from prison, and lynched him.

The writer feels like offering an apology to the
reader for inserting the following newspaper article
on Walker's case, because of its utter fiendishness;
but in view of the fact that the woman did not
charge him with attempted rape, he believes that
nothing could better reveal the deplorable condition
of life in the South than this same article.   Here
it is : —

"" The *Memphis Commercial* of Sunday, July 23,
contains a full account of the tragedy from which
the following extracts are made,

At 12 o'clock last night, Lee Walker, who
attempted to outrage Miss Mollie McCadden, last
Tuesday morning, was taken from the county jail
and hanged to a telegraph pole just north of the
prison.   All day rumors were afloat that with
nightfall an attack would be made upon the jail,
and as everyone anticipated that a vigorous resist-
ance would be made, a conflict between the mob
and the authorities was feared.

At 10 o'clock Capt. O'Haver, Sergt. Horan and
several patrolmen were on hand, but they could do
nothing with the crowd.   An attack by the mob was
made on the door in the south wall and it yielded.

At 12 o'clock the door of the prison was broken in
with a rail.

As soon as the rapist was brought out of the door,
calls were heard for a rope ; then some one shouted
' Burn him ! ' But there was no time to make a fire.
When Walker got into the lobby a dozen of the men
began beating and stabbing him. He was half
dragged, half carried to the corner of Front street
and the alley between Sycamore and Mill, and hung
to a telephone pole.

The mob proceeded north on Front street with the
victim, stopping at Sycamore street to get a rope
from a grocery. ' Take him to the iron bridge on
Main street,' yelled several men. The men who
had hold of the Negro were in a hurry to finish the
job, however, and when they reached the telephone
pole at the corner of Front street and the first alley
north of Sycamore they stopped. A hastily improv-
ised noose was slipped over the Negro's head and
several young men mounted a pile of lumber near
the pole and threw the rope over one of the iron
stepping pins. The Negro was lifted up until his
feet were three feet above the ground, the rope was
made taut, and a corpse dangled in mid-air. A big
fellow who helped lead the mob pulled the Negro's
legs until his neck cracked. The wretch's clothes
had been torn off, and, as he swung, the man who
pulled his legs mutilated the corpse.

One or two knife cuts, more or less, made little
difference in the appearance of the dead rapist, however, for before the rope was around his neck his
skin was cut almost to ribbons. One pistol shot
was fired while the corpse was hanging. A dozen

voices protested against the use of firearms, and there was no more shooting. The body was permitted to hang for half an hour, then it was cut down and the rope divided among those who lingered around the scene of the tragedy. Then it was suggested that the corpse be burned, and it was done. The entire performance, from the assault on the jail to the burning of the dead Negro was witnessed by a score or so of policemen and as many deputy sheriffs, but not a hand was lifted to stop the proceedings after the jail door yielded.

Detective Richardson, who is also a deputy coroner, then proceeded to impanel the following jury of inquest: J. S. Moody, A. C. Waldran, B. J. Childs, J. N. House, Nelson Bills, T. L. Smith, and A. Newhouse. After viewing the body the inquest was adjourned without any testimony being taken until 9 o'clock this morning. The jury will meet at the coroner's office, 51 Beale street, upstairs, and decide on a verdict. If no witnesses are forthcoming, the jury will be able to arrive at a verdict just the same, as all members of it saw the lynching. Then some one raised the cry of ' Burn him ! ' It was quickly taken up and soon resounded from a hundred throats. Detective Richardson for a long time, single handed, stood the crowd off. He talked and begged the men not to bring disgrace on the city by burning the body, arguing that all the vengeance possible had been wrought.

While this was going on a small crowd was busy starting a fire in the middle of the street. The material was handy. Some bundles of staves were taken from the adjoining lumber yard for kindling.

Heavier wood was obtained from the same source, and coal oil from a neighboring grocery. Then the cries of ' Burn him! Burn him! ' were redoubled. Half a dozen men seized the naked body. The crowd cheered. They marched to the fire, and giving the body a swing, it was landed in the middle of the fire. There was a cry for more wood, as the fire had begun to die owing to the long delay. Willing hands procured the wood, and it was piled up on the Negro, almost, for a time, obscuring him from view. The head was in plain view, as also were the limbs, and one arm which stood out high above the body, the elbow crooked, held in that position by a stick of wood. In a few moments the hands began to swell, then came great blisters over all the exposed parts of the body ; then in places the flesh was burned away and the bones began to show through. It was a horrible sight, one which perhaps none there had ever witnessed before. It proved too much for a large part of the crowd and the majority of the mob left very shortly after the burning began.

The rope that was used to hang the Negro, and also that which was used to lead him from the jail, were eagerly sought by relic-hunters. They almost fought for a chance to cut off a piece of rope, and in an incredably short time both ropes had dis- appeared and were scattered in the pockets of the crowd in sections of from an inch to six inches long. Others of the relic-hunters remained until the ashes cooled to obtain such ghastly relics as the teeth, nails and bits of charred skin of the im- molated victim of his own lust. After burning the body the mob tied a rope around the charred trunk and dragged it down Main street to the Court House, where it was hanged to a center pole. The rope broke and the corpse dropped with a thud, but it was again hoisted, the charred legs barely touching the ground. The teeth were knocked out and the finger nails cut off as souvenirs. The crowd made so much noise that the police interfered. Undertaker Walsh was telephoned for, who took charge of the body and carried it to his establishment, where it will be prepared for burial in the potter's field to-day.''

It is impossible to describe the loathsomeness of this revolting murder. It is enough to say it was done in the open, in the presence of representatives of the law, and without so much as identification of the man by the woman.

Mr. R. C. O. Benjamin, Attorney at Law, in his pamphlet '' Southern Outrages,'' affords much information. The following quotations will tell their own story : —

'' NEW ORLEANS, September 17th, 1893. — Three Negroes were lynched in the parish of Jefferson at midnight Saturday. Since the murder of Judge Victor Estopinal on Friday by the Negro Julien, excitement has been at high pitch in that parish and parties of white men on foot and on horses have been scouting the country looking for the murderer. The searching parties became very much aroused

when the murderer could not be found. On the
suspicion of conspiracy Julien's three brothers,
Valsin, Bazile, and Paul, and two cousins, with
the murderer's mother, and the wives and sisters of
the other men were arrested and locked up in the
jail at Southport Wharf, a mile from New Orleans.
Late last night the mob disappointed at the failure
to find the murderer ('Julien') broke into the Jail.
There was a proposition to lynch five of the male
prisoners, but this was over-ruled and only two,
Bazile and Valsin, were lynched and the cousins
severely whipped and ordered out of the parish.
The mob took the remaining brother, Paul, to Camp
Parapet, a settlement consisting almost entirely of
Negroes, a few miles away, where he was lynched
to over-awe the Negroes. All three men were
strangled to death. After Valsin and Bazile had
been taken out of the jail they were carried across
to a pasture one hundred yards away, and there
were offered the chance to save their lives by telling
where their brother was. The Negroes made no
reply. · They were then told to kneel and pray. One
did so, the other remained standing. Both prayed
fervently. The taller Negro was then hoisted up.
He remained hanging five minures before the second
was hanged. The shorter Negro stood gazing at his
dying brother without flinching. It is said that the
reason the women were arrested was because they

were found wrapping up some clothing and a loaf of bread. This caused suspicion that the articles were to be conveyed to the fugitive murderer.

During the search for Julien on Saturday, a part of the mob visited the house of a Negro family in the neighbourhood of Camp Parapet, and failing to find the murderer they were looking for, tried to induce John Willis, a young Negro, to tell where he was. Willis could not do so, not knowing, and he was kicked to death by the gang. During the day it was reported that Judge Long, Judge Estopinal's predecessor was assaulted by a Negro. For this two Negroes were lynched and a large number whipped and ordered out of the parish. A victim of this phase of their barbarism, named William Sams was put in jail at Kenner, Jefferson Parish. He suffered terribly from the torture he received. Describing the man's experience the *Dispatch* says ; His feet were swollen, and all about the region of the toes and instep were streaks of white or dead skin, which showed out in strong contrast against the natural skin. A bundle of papers was set a fire and placed beneath his feet; then while it burned the regulators stood around and attempted to extract confessions as to the whereabouts of Julien. Finding they could get no confession out of him they put him in the jail and claimed that he built a fire in the cell and tortured himself. He was afterwards lynched for the awful crime of torturing himself.

The mob determined to find the murderer, (Julien) got blood hounds from the penitentiary and let them loose in swamps where it was supposed the murderer was in hiding, meanwhile the mob sent word to the agent of the State's laws that when the Negro was found they intended to burn him in broad day light. On the spot where Judge Estopinal fell and died an iron stake was driven into the ground, to which he was to be tied. Fat pine and resinous materials surrounded this. Long iron like branding irons, were put in readiness with which he was to be tortured, while the fire underneath him burned. A rude gallows tree above the pyre was built from which he was to be suspended. The preparations were not in vain, the unfortunate man was caught and dealt with in a manner by these white men of Louisiana, that Apache Indians would be ashamed of. And the guardians of the peace stood and looked on complacently while justice was outraged at the very door of her temple. In the whole annals of race crimes in the South, and at the time when political passions were burning most fiercely, we remember no occurrence as astrocius as the murder of the three innocent Negroes in Jefferson Parish, Louisiana, September, 1893. Even the daily press of New Orleans, which so often condoned lynching, spoke out boldly against this act of barbarity. The *Picayune*, always timid and conservative, was the first to lead. While it made reports of the barbarous transaction that little tallied with the real facts, it yet spoke against those outrages. It said in its Sunday edition (September 17th) :

" Whatever may have been their (the Julien brothers') connection with the case, so far, there is no reason to believe that they were privy to the murder of Judge Estopinal, and, therefore, the *Picayune* cannot find any justification for this lynching. On the contrary, it must be condemned. The *Picayune* realizes that there was and should be a most intense popular indignation against the murderer . . . but to take the lives of the other parties under the circumstances cannot be justified. It is a reflection on the officials and citizens whose administration of justice and execution of the law are so lax as to have destroyed public confidence in them. It is the height of savagery to butcher people who are guilty of no offense, but are only suspected and it only shows the fearful extremes of lawlessness to which the country is rapidly drifting."

The Times Democrat agreeably surprised many, and spoke boldly. In the course of its remarks it said :

" These three men who have been lynched were, as far as known, absolutely unconnected with the crime of their brother. There is not a title of evidence, not a tenable suspicion even, that they had any hand in the killing of Judge Estopinal, or that they even sympathized in that diabolical deed. The killing of the three men, therefore, under the circumstances, for the sole reason presumably that the bloodthirsty avengers, baffled in their pursuit of the murderer, must wreak their spite on some of his kin, however innocent, must be set down as one of the most monstrous deeds that have ever disgraced and humilated this part of the country. It is unmittigated cruelty, cowardice and barbarism from beginning to end, without so much as one redeaming feature in it. Much is at any time to be excused to a justly aroused and enraged community ; but there is no excuse to be made for white men calling themselves gentlemen, who deliberately take out the innocent relatives of a murderer, knowing them to be innocent, and kill them like dogs on the mere ground of their blood relationship.''

"PARIS, TEXAS, February 1st, 1893. — A more horrible death than that which was meted out to Henry Smith, the colored ravisher and murderer of little Myrtle Vance, in this city to-day history does not record. The execution of a Negro at Texarkana, (Ed. Coy), several months ago pales to insignificance compared with the awful torture to which Smith was subjected. When the news of his capture flashed over the wires last evening, those who felt that no fate was too cruel for the Negro, set about preparing for his execution in a manner calculated to strike terror to the Negro element of Texas by making a horrible example of Smith. To such an extreme was the desire to wreak vengeance on the doomed Negro gratified that the entire civilized world may stand aghast at the manner of his execution. It was no spontaneous affair, but had been carefully planned and was executed in its most appalling details in a manner calculated to recall scenes of the Dark Ages. When the train bearing the condemned Negro arrived, not only every member of the community, was in waiting at the depot to receive him and attend his execution, but there were thousands gathered from all towns within a radius of a hundred miles of Paris. Smith's appearance was greeted with wild cheers. There were no efforts to summarily dispose of him. A slow lingering death awaited him, which for downright torture finds few parallels in the history of the martyrs. After being placed in a wagon, Smith, trembling and livid with fear, was driven to the place where death in awful form awaited him . . .

Out on the bare prairie where stood scattering Bois d'Arcs shrubs the scaffold had been built. Four uprights supported, ten feet above ground, a platform ten feet square, railed in except on the south side where a stair ascended. In its center a strong post was set and braced on either side. As the wagon approached, Henry Vance, the father of Smith's victim, appeared on the platform and asked the crowd, now densely packed for hundreds of yards away and numbering ten thousand people, to be quiet, that he wanted for a while to get his revenge, and then he would turn the prisoner over to any one that wanted him.

Here came the wagon, and Smith was carried onto the platform, stripped to the waist and placed against the stake. His legs, arms and body were corded to it, and he was delivered over to Vance's vengeance to expiate his crime.

A tinner's furnace was brought on filled with irons heated white. Taking one, Vance thrust it under one and then the other side of his victim's feet, who, helpless, writhed as the flesh scarred and peeled from the bones. Slowly, inch by inch, up his legs the irons were drawn and re-drawn, only the nervous, jerky twist of the muscles showing the agony being endured. When his body was reached and the iron was pressed to its most tender part he broke silence for the first time and a prolonged scream of agony rent the air. Slowly across and around the body, slowly upward traced the irons, the withered, seared flesh marking the progress of the awful punishment.

By turns Smith screamed, prayed, begged and cursed his torturer.

When his face was reached his tongue was

silenced by fire, and thenceforth he only moaned or gave a cry that echoed over the prairie like the wail of a wild animal. Then his eyes were put out, and not a finger's breadth of his body being unscathed his executioners gave way.

They were Vance, his brother-in-law and Vance's son, a boy fifteen years of age. When they gave over punishing Smith they left the platform.

Smith and the clothing about his lower limbs were then saturated with oil as was the platform. The space beneath was filled with combustibles, and the whole was covered with oil, and fire simultaneously set to his feet and the stack below.

A cold, sleeting rain had been falling since noon. Silhouetted against the dark, leaden sky, the platform loomed tall and gaunt, and above it with his head dropped on his breast, blackened and scorched, was the body, and so still was it that all thought him dead. Slowly the flames wrapped him in their bluish veil. A moment they burned so and then a shudder shook the throng. The head slowly raised and a broken, quivering cry broke the breathless silence, and was echoed back by shouts and cries from the more thoughtless below.

Then the cords binding the arms burned and he raised the crisped and blackened stumps to wipe the sightless sockets of his eyes.

Then the cords about his waist burned, and he

toppled forward upon the platform and laid there
writhing and quivering in the greedy flames. One
foot was still fast and held him on a bed of flame.

With one supreme effort the body, still animated
by the supreme desire of escape, rolled over on its
face, rose upon its arms, reached up and caught
the railing, and with convulsive efforts tore the
bound leg loose, and stood reeling on the stumps
of its feet.

It dragged itself nearly upright against the railing and then dropped sitting upon the burning
platform, its head and arms lying upon the railing
and the legs dangling over the edge, and there
hung a moment as though this had nearly exhausted
its little strength.

Then, as the flames roared around him, by another effort he slipped over the egde and fell to the
ground. The body lay there still, but was thrust
into the mass of fire from beneath the scaffold from
which it came, in a few minutes crawling out only
to be thrust back again, and the debris of the fire
was piled on top and so did death come to Henry
Smith.

Every scrap of his clothing was eagerly sought
by relic hunters, and when the flames had at length
died away, the charred fragments of his bones were
raked out and carried away.''

At Bardwell, Kentucky, C. J. Miller was lynched

July seventh, 1893. On July fith two white girls were found murdered, and their bodies mutilated, but no satisfactory clue to the author of the tragedy could be found. In any society governed by laws of civilization detectives would have been set to work and every effort made to find the murderer ; but the people of Bardwell jumped to the conclusion that a Negro had done the foul deed, and at once began to look for one. Miller was arrested in Sikeston, Missouri, and was handed over to the authorities of Kentucky. He gave his right name without hesitation, and an account of his movements from the first to the fifth of July, the latter date being that of the murder. He said : " My name is C. J. Miller. I am of Springfield, Illinois. My wife lives at 716, North Second Street. I am here among you to-day looked upon as one of the most brutal men before the people. I stand here surrounded by men who are excited ; men who are not willing to let the law take its course, and as far as the law is concerned, I have committed no crime, and certainly no crime gross enough to deprive me of my life or liberty to walk upon the green earth. I had some rings which I bought in Bismarck of a Jew peddler. I paid him $4.50 for them. I left Springfield on the first day of July and came to Alton. From Alton I went to East St. Louis, from there to Jefferson Barracks, thence to De Soto, thence to Bismarck; and to Piedmont, thence to Poplar Bluff, thence to Hoxie, to Jonesboro, and then on a local freight to Malden, from there to Sikeston. On the fifth day of July, the day I was supposed to have committed the offence, I was at Bismarck."

No statement of a man's movements could be clearer, and nothing might have been easier for the police to investigate. One visit to Bismarck would have been sufficient to clear the Negro of the charge, or to have cast suspicion on his story. No investigation was made. The mob took him by force from the jail, tore off his clothing, and hanged him to a telegraph pole. Within twelve hours of his arrest he was a dead man with toes and fingers cut off. After his murder his statement was proven true.

The lynchings of 1894, — in number, one hundred and ninety-four — were of the usual order. Innocent men and women, and men and women who were guilty of crime, whom the *law* ought to have punished in a just manner, were taken from the field, their homes, and state jails and done to death, and police and authorities looked on the brutal work, perhaps unable to prevent it. When the law connot be enforced, social order is surely not much different from that of savage tribes, with which observation we leave the year 1894.

On the sixteenth of November, 1895, a young lady

named Miss Jones was found in an unconscious condition in the garden of her home at 6 o'clock in the
evening. At 8 o'clock the city policeman arrested
a Negro named James Goings, and placed him in
the jail. At once a rumour of Negro outrage was
spread through the town, which was Frederick,
North Dakota, and as the night wore on a crowd
gathered and became too large for the authorities
to handle, and at midnight they attacked the jail
and took Goings out in his underclothing, a lawyer,
a newspaper man and other prominent citizens being
the leaders. Half-an-hour later Goings was hanging from a chestnut tree near the town, on which
a Negro was hanged in November, 1887. When
the *untried* and *unrecognized* man had been safely
"swung up" the lynchers amused themselves by
shooting at him. Such brutality causes despair of
heart, also amazement that a civilized country can
permit it to be done.

At Gilson, Glasscock County, on November 21,
1895, Balam Hancock, a Negro, was lynched before
day light. For what? Miss Dessie Shelton, a girl
seventeen years old, said he had *tried* to assault
her. *Rightly enough* the police on receipt of the
report set out to find him, and eventually he was
caught in Jefferson County and lodged in jail.
Not one word will be found in this book in the way
of apology for wrong doing, indeed we say with all

earnestness, arrest and punish severely every man who attempts to violate the honour of our wives and daughters; but let justice be done. It is one of the best known facts of life in the Southern States that white men constantly outrage black women, and that never a word is spoken about the matter. Balam Hancock *attempted* outrage, — it was said, but not proven — and was arrested and placed in jail, and then by force taken therefrom and hanged to a tree. We would ask this question. If a black man is a brute when he attempts outrage, and merits death, what are the white men who hang him without trial, and what do *they* deserve?

Joe Robinson and Ozias McGalvey, both coloured, were tried at Nashville, Tennessee, November, 1895, for rape, and were found guilty and sentenced to twenty-one years imprisonment. On the twenty-ninth November they were put in charge of some prison officers and sent by train for Tracy City, which they never reached. A Nashville mob wired someone at Fayetteville, who at once called out the lynchers of that town, who in their turn, acting on the instructions of the telegram, went to the railway station, waited for the train, and when it arrived took the prisoners by force and lodged them in the jail. Meanwhile the Nashville mob had taken train for Fayetteville, where in due time they arrived, took the Negroes from the jail and hanged them at

8 o'clock in the court-yard, which, be it observed, is the county seat of Lincoln County. These men had been duly tried, found guilty, and most properly sentenced by the judge ; but what can the people of Tennessee say for the government of that state? If these lynched men had been *white* instead of *black*, and if *coloured* men had been the lynchers, no Negro's life in the state would have been worth a day's purchase. We say they were rightly sentenced to a long imprisonment ; but can not keep back this observation — let not American citizens boast of their civilization until they shall have asserted and established the justice, equality and majesty of American law.

At Rockfield, Kentucky, February 5, 1897, a most revolting display of savagery was witnessd. Robert Morton, of course a coloured man, was guilty of writing an insulting letter to Miss Johnson, a young white woman of some repute who lived at Rockfield. We do *not* know what the punishment for writing insulting letters is in Kentucky, but it is quite clear that Kentucky mobs hold it is *death for Negroes*. The police took him to a house on the Russelville road, and left him in charge of a *sufficient* guard, whence he was taken at midnight and hanged. Nothing could be more barbarous than this. Pandemonium, the *fabled* hall of demons, is horrid enough to imagine ; bnt here is a *real* pandemonium, and demons who seem to delight in imbruing their hands in the human blood of their fellow-citizens.

On the eighteenth of February, 1897, about eight miles from Roxie, Mississippi, a murder was committed of the most dastardly nature. Ben Land, a coloured man, and his wife lived on a piece of United States land, which by hard, continuous labour they had improved. Late at night, when he and his wife were asleep, armed men surrounded his little home, sprinkled it with coal oil, set it on fire, and waited. Soon the place was enveloped in flames, and poor Land and his wife rushed out into the darkness to save their lives. She *did* escape; but he was shot down the moment he emerged from his burning home, and was found next morning "with all the top and back of his head shot off." His only offence was living on that particular piece of land, which was proven in the State's Court. He was known as a quiet, industrious man, and lived on terms of peace and good-will with everybody. The fact is, a white family wanted the property and had approached Land in respect of it, who, having consulted Hon. S. A. Beadle, an attorney-at-law, intended compromising with them, because he knew that henceforth his life would not be safe. He was not allowed to live long enough to carry out his purpose. He was murdered, and his wife was turned out to do as best she could, and white men saw the deed done, — *did it* — and went on their way in a *Christian Country*.

We have given this account of these lynchings in the briefest manner, and have striven to avoid the use of inflammatory language. They tell their own story, and are a fearful reflection on the social condition of life in the South of the United States. Sixteen hundred and ninety-seven coloured men, women and children have been lynched to death in the last fifteen years, and other outrages on the race have been perpetrated, more than can be counted. It has been enough for a white man to make a charge against a black man to cause the mob to arrange punishment, or a lynching, and legal officials have been powerless to prevent them. For attempted rape, for suspected murder, for marrying a white person, and for no reason given, these lynchings have been done in defiance of law, and the spirit which did them obtains at *this hour* in the South. If a white man commit rape on a black woman no notice is taken of it, not even by the police, and these murders in the light of day are done without any attempt being made to punish the murderers. Lynch Law might as well be written into the constitution of many states ; it *is* in force and *flourishes* in not a few of them. Public opinion, if there be such a thing on this question, is impotent, and can avail nothing, which terrible fact ought to stir the churches of both North and South to begin a campaign of education, and of denunciation. '' How long, O Lord, how long '' shall this horror continue? When will Thy coloured children be properly recognized and treated humanly by Thy white children?

When the white men of the South left their homes to join the army and fight the North, the coloured slave was left in charge, and not a single case of outrage has been reported against him ; none during the whole war period ; none to this day. Wives, children, and property were left behind, and he, in thousands of cases, was the only man about to sow and gather harvests, and protect the home. He laboured, and obeyed, and suffered the indignity of a slave's condition as in former years, yet never attempted outrage ; but now he is free this charge is made against him indiscriminately. It may be that a few black men, which is equally true of a few white men, have wickedly made the attempt ; but the law ought to deal with them, and their punishment should be inflicted in a civilized manner. No christian would shield a fiend, be he white or black, guilty of indecent attacks upon women ; but a trial at law is the right of both black and white. What would white men say and do, if black men lynched *one of them ?* Not for a day would they suffer such a condition of things. The

Negro is in the minority, is weak, is disliked, and can be shot or lynched; but the day is coming when this last abomination shall be banished from the South by the force of public opinion. White Southerners there are in thousands who regret the crimes which are done, who labour day by day to create a more humane condition of thought, and if there be a God of truth and compassion, which cannot be doubted, their labours cannot be in vain; they must succeed.

HON. JUDGE GEORGE L. RUFFIN.

CHAPTER IX.

THE NEGRO OF THE NORTH.

Before and since emancipation the Northern States have accorded the Negro many advantages and opportunities of progress, which the States of the South have until now with-held from him; and, as might be expected, in the North he is far more independent of spirit, and disposed to take a lively interest in public affairs. Here he is among friends, who recognize him in the spirit of humanity. He attends, if he so desire, the white man's church; sends his children to the ordinary common school; sells his labour in the open market; takes a part in politics; can ride in the white man's car; is free to enjoy the privileges of the constitution.

He is, we say, among friends in the North; but *all* the inhabitants are not his friends, neither does he enjoy equality of opportunity. Some are yet unfriendly to him, and many places are closed against him, which may be filled by white men only. Not many white men call him to exercise his medical skill upon them, and perhaps none resort to him for legal advice; in the higher branches of labour he must find employment among coloured people, or not at all. Therefore, his freedom to compete in every field of enterprise is considerably impaired, and in many directions rendered useless.

Of this disadvantage complaint is useless; time must work the remedy, and will. Patience and perseverance must be his companions; faith in the good providence of God must dwell in his heart. Strife will not help him; but education, thrift and practice of religion will break down the wall of exclusion, and in due time he and his friends will rejoice in a perfect victory. In the North it depends entirely upon himself whether he finally stand abreast with his white brother or remain in his present position.

In this connection we must look backward. For the last hundred and thirty years the Negro has been making it manifest that he is endowed with soul faculties, which he has used to great advantage, thanks to the inspiring sympathy of friends. He has invented labour-saving machinery, written books, composed music, acquired and used eloquence of speech, built churches and Sunday-schools, and published volumes of poetry; in almost every department of human effort in the North he has distinguished himself.

Far back as the year 1761 a slave-ship arrived at Boston from Africa, and among the slaves was a delicate girl of seven years. She had, of course, been stolen from her mother, probably by another Negro, who no doubt sold her to a white dealer on the coast. At the sale, which was held soon after her arrival in Boston, she was bought by Mr. John Wheatley for his wife, who, requiring a girl, attended the slave auction and selected her because she was delicate and graceful in appearance. Mrs. Wheatley gave her the name of Phillis and treated her with motherly affection, also educated her, and was soon repaid with most grateful service and with tokens of genius and superiority of intellect which surprised everybody who visited her house.

In less than a year and a half from the time of her importation she could converse fluently in English,—which language she had not heard before being kidnapped — and could read and pronounce correctly the most difficult passages of scripture ; and within a period of ten years she wrote letters and poetry that astonished the literary men of New England. The growth of her piety kept pace with that of her intelligence ; she learned to fear and love God most devoutly, and became a communicant of the Old South Church under the simple name of " Phillis, the servant of Mr. Wheatley." Having no paternal name of her own, she was too scrupulous to have her master's name written on the church register as her surname.

In 1773 she was sent to England for the benefit of her health with Mr. Nathaniel Wheatley and his family, and was well received in London, where her poems were published. The following letter — selected as a sample — reveals the quality of her piety and intelligence.

"TO OBOUR TANNER, IN NEW PORT.

Boston Oct. 30, 1773

Dear Obour, — I rec'd your most kind epistles of Augt. 27th, and Oct. 13th, by a young man of your acquaintance, for which I am oblig'd to you.   I hear of your welfare with pleasure; but this acquaints you that I am at present indispos'd by a cold, and since my arrival have been visited by the asthma.

Your observations on our dependence on the Deity, and your hopes that my wants will be supply'd from his fulness which is in Christ Jesus, is truly worthy of yourself.   I can't say but my voyage to England has conduced to the recovery (in a great measure) of my health.   The friends I found there among the nobility and gentry, their benevolent conduct towards me, the unexpected and unmerited civility and complaisance with which I was treated by all, fills me with astonishment.   I can scarcely realize it.   This I humbly hope has the happy effect of lessening me in my own esteem. Your reflections on the sufferings of the Son of God, and the inestimable price of our immortal souls,

plainly demonstrate the sensations of a soul united
to Jesus. What you observe of Esau is true of all
mankind, who (left to themselves) would sell their
heavenly birth rights for a few moments of sensual
pleasure, whose wages at last (dreadful wages!) is
eternal condemnation. Dear Obour, let us not sell
our birthright for a thousand worlds, which indeed
would be as dust upon the balance. The God of
the seas and dry land, has graciously brought me
home in safety. Join with me in thanks to him for
so great a mercy, and that it may excite me to praise
him with cheerfulness, to preserve in Grace and
Faith, and in the knowledge of our Creator and
Redeemer,—that my heart may be fill'd with gratitude. I should have been pleas'd greatly to see
Miss West, as I imagine she knew you. I have
been very busy ever since my arrival, or should
have now wrote a more particular account of my
voyage, but must submit that satisfaction to some
other opportunity. I am Dear friend,
            Most affectionately ever yours
                    PHILLIS WHEATLEY

My mistress has been sick above 14 weeks, and
confined to her bed the whole time, but I hope is
somewhat better, now.
The young man by whom this is handed you
seems to me to be a very clever man, knows you
very well, and is very complaisant and agreeable.
I enclose Proposals for my book,* and beg you'd
use your interest to get subscriptions, as it is for
my benefit.   P. W."

*This refers to the first edition of Phillis' collected poems, which
was printed in London, in 1773.

Her letters, however, though very beautiful, caused no excitement in the literary world ; but her poems, of which she composed thirty-nine, which were published by Mr. A. Bell, Bookseller, No. 8, near the Saracens Head, Aldgate, London, created so much astonishment that it became necessary for the following statement to be made to convince the public that they were the productions of a slave girl : —

"We whose names are under-written, do assure the world, that the poems specified in the following pages, were (as we verily believe) written by Phillis, a young Negro girl, who was but a few years since, brought an uncultivated Barbarian from Africa, and has ever since been, and now is, under the dis-advantage of serving as a slave in a family in this town. She has been examined by some of the best judges, and is thought qualified to write them.

His Excellency Thomas Hutchinson, Governor ; The Hon. Andrew Oliver, Lieutenant-Governor ; The Hon. Thomas Hubbard ; The Hon. John Erving ; The Hon. James Pitts ; The Hon. Harri-son Gray ; The Hon. James Bowdoin ; The Rev. Charles Chenney, D. D. ; The Rev. Mather Byles, D. D. ; The Rev. Ed. Pemberton, D. D. ; The Rev. Andrew Eliot, D. D. ; The Rev. Samuel Cooper, D. D. ; John Hancock, Esq. ; Joseph Green, Esq. ; Richard Carey, Esq. ; Mr. Samul Mather ; Mr. John Moorhead ; Mr. John Wheatley, her master."

Her master also published a letter in confirmation of above statement.

The two quotations given below must suffice, and will show the quality of her work.

ON BEING BROUGHT FROM AFRICA TO AMERICA.

" 'T was mercy brought me from my Pagan land,
Taught my benighted soul to understand
That there's a God, that there's a Saviour too;
Once I redemption neither sought nor knew.
Some view our sable race with scornful eye,
   ' Their colour is a diabolic die.'
Remember, Christians, Negroes, black as Cain,
May be refin'd, and join th' Angelic train."

The following is selected from a poem of about one hundred lines.

ON VIRTUE.

"O thou bright jewel in my aim I strive
To comprehend thee.   Thine own words declare
Wisdom is higher than a fool can reach.
I cease to wonder, and no more attempt
Thine height t' explore, or fathom thy profound.
But, O my soul, sink not into despair,
Virtue is near thee, and with gentle hand
Would now embrace thee, hovers o'er thine head.
Fain would the heav'n-born soul with her converse,
Then seek, then court her for her promis'd bliss."

A Negro of the North; a child of God; a minister of His grace; a sweet singer of divine thoughts; a link which bound the *coloured slave* to the *white owner* on the highest plain of life; one that gave proof to the world of the common origin of the human race was Phillis Wheatley.

In the year 1817 Frederick Douglass was born a slave in the district of Tuckahoe, Maryland, whence he was transferred to Baltimore, Maryland, where he lived seven years, and then ran away and sought safety and liberty in the North.

At Baltimore he found a friend in his owner's wife, who taught him letters and in many ways endeavoured to help him acquire knowledge. But this tender-hearted mistress had not remembered her husband in all this human helpfulness, and was surprised by being told it was against the interest of slave-owners to educate their slaves; her good work was stopped there and then. But the mind of young Douglass could not be so easily kept in the darkness of ignorance as his owner's wife could be stopped giving him instruction; having tasted the sweet of knowledge he *must* and *did* continue the pursuit of it. And as he made progress he was better able to estimate rightly the painful experiences of slavery — early separation from his mother, whippings, scarcity of clothing, lack of school and church, etc., etc. — which experiences filled his

EDWIN G. WALKER, ESQ., ATTORNEY AT LAW.
HE WAS ELECTED TO THE MASSACHUSETTS LEGISLATURE IN 1863 AND
NOMINATED BY GENERAL BUTLER FOR THE POSITION OF JUDGE.

mind with thoughts that burned within and demanded expression.

In this condition he arrived at New York, a fugitive slave, where he was assisted by a coloured
gentleman, Mr. David Ruggles. At New York he
married his first wife, who was a *free* coloured
woman, from whom he was liable at any moment to
be taken and sent back into slavery. However, his
friend shielded and guided him, and ultimately sent
him to New Bedford, Massachusetts, where he
found new friends to help and credit with which to
start life afresh, also work at a brass foundry, which
he followed earnestly and patiently. In a little
while he became an exhorter in the Coloured
Methodist Church, and soon earned a good reputa-
tion, which fact really determined his life work, as
we shall see.

At that time William Lloyd Garrison was issuing
every week powerful arguments against slavery in
the " Liberator " — a copy of which Douglas never
failed to secure — and was holding meetings North,
South, East, and West of New England. In the
summer of 1841, at Nantucket, Massachusetts, an
anti-slavery convention was held, which was attended by abolitionists from Boston, Worcester,
New Bedford, and many cities of New England,
William Lloyd Garrison presiding. Douglass heard
of this convention, and decided to attend it, which

decision was the turning point of his life. Man
never knows how much depends upon apparently
insignificant actions.

In the immense audience which had assembled
to hear William Lloyd Garrison, and to discuss the
question of slavery was William C. Coffin of New
Bedford, who had heard Douglass make earnest
appeals to sinners in the Coloured Methodist
Church, who also had an idea that the young slave
— Douglass was yet a slave — might very well
help the good cause by using his exhorting power
before that assembly. He sought Douglass out
and urged him to speak, and succeeded, from which
moment a New sphere opened to the "fugitive
slave," whose influence against slavery became
second to that of Mr. Garrison only. He was engaged by the Anti-Slavery Society as an agent, and
was sent on a lecturing tour through New England.
His appearance created a great sensation, and the
thousands who flocked to hear him were astounded
by his eloquence. "A *thing* that can *talk* and give
an interesting account of the cruelties of slavery,"
— was the favorite advertisement of his meetings,
and the "thing that can talk" so astonished the
hearers that many were with difficulty convinced he
was a slave. However, a slave he was, and on his
head was a price, which would have had to be paid,
if his owner in Baltimore, Maryland, had known

that Frederick Douglass the orator was the nameless slave who had run away from him, or
Frederick Douglass could have been forced back
into slavery.   Indeed the price was paid while
Douglass was in England.   Mrs. Henry Richardson
and a few friends raised the money, purchased his
liberty, and placed his freedom papers in his hands.

This remarkable man, who once had to hide himself in New York from slave-catchers, became a
Presidential Elector for the state of New York, and
voted in the name of that state for U. S. Grant, in
1872 ; was sometime United States Marshall for the
District of Columbia ;   Recorder of Deeds for the
same district under President Garfield ;   edited
several newspapers and published a few books; and,
after a life of extraordinary activity, passed into
rest in the year 1896, leaving a character behind
that will endure in the memory of humanity.

The following quotations will enable the reader
to estimate the mental power of this " *Thing that
can talk.*"

Writing to Mr. Garrison on the 1st of January,
1846, from England, he said, among other things : —

" *My dear friend Garrison*, — Up to this time I
have given no direct expression of the views, feelings, and opinions which I have formed, respecting
the character and condition of the people of this
land.   I have refrained thus, purposely.   I wish to

speak advisedly, and in order to do this, I have
waited till, I trust, experience has brought my
opinions to an intelligent maturity. . . . I can
truly say, I have spent some of the happiest moments
of my life since landing in this country. I seem to
have undergone a transformation. I live a new
life. . . . The deep sympathy for the slave, and
the strong abhorrence of the slave-holder, everywhere evinced; the cordiality with which members
and ministers of religious bodies, and of various
shades of religious opinion, have embraced me, and
lent me their aid; the kind hospitality constantly
proffered me by persons of the highest rank in
society; the spirit of freedom that seems to animate
all with whom I have come in contact, and the entire
absence of everything that looked like prejudice
against me, on account of the colour of my skin —
contrasted so strongly with my long and bitter
experience in the United States, that I look with
wonder and amazement on the transition. . . .
I gaze around in vain for one who will question my
equal humanity, claim me as his slave, or offer me
an insult. . . . I find no difficulty here in obtain-
ing admission into any place of worship, instruction,
or amusement, on equal terms with people as white
as any I ever saw in the United States. I meet
nothing to remind me of my complexion. I find
myself regarded and treated at every turn with the
kindness and deference paid to white people. When
I go to church, I am met by no upturned nose and
scornful lip to tell me, ' We don't allow Niggers in
here.' ''

On the fifth of July, 1852, at Rochester, New York, he made the following remarks in what is considered the most effective speech of his life, on the subject of American Independence : —

" *Fellow Citizens :* — Pardon me, and allow me to ask, why am I called upon to speak here to-day ? What have I, or those I represent, to do with your national independence ? Are the great principles of political freedom and of natural justice embodied in that declaration of Independence, extended to us? And am I, therefore, called upon to bring our humble offering to the national altar, and to confess the benefits, and express devout gratitude for the blessings resulting from your independence to us ? Would to God, both for your sakes and ours, that an affirmative answer could be truthfully returned to these questions ! Then would my task be light, and my burden easy and delightful. . . . This Fourth of July is *yours*, not *mine*. *You* may rejoice, I must mourn. To drag a man in fetters into the grand illuminated temple of liberty, and call upon him to join you in joyous anthems, were inhuman mockery and sacrilegious irony. . . . Fellow citizens, above your national, tumultuous joy, I hear the mournful wail of millions, whose chains, heavy and grievous yesterday, are to-day rendered more intolerable by the jubilant shouts that reach them. If I do forget, if I do not faithfully remember those

bleeding children of sorrow this day, ' may my right
hand forget her cunning, and may my tongue cleave
to the roof of my mouth.' . . . My subject, then,
fellow citizens, is American Slavery. I do not hesitate to declare, with all my soul, that the character
and conduct of this nation never looked blacker to
me than on this Fourth of July. America is false
to the past, false to the present, and solemnly binds
herself to be false to the future. Standing with
God and the crushed and bleeding slave on this
occasion, I will, in the name of humanity which is
outraged, in the name of liberty which is fettered,
in the name of the Constitution and the Bible, which
are disregarded and trampled upon, dare to call in
question and denounce, with all the emphasis I can
command, everything that serves to perpetuate
slavery — the great sin and shame of America.''

It is more than probable that many of his audience, who were present to celebrate the Fourth of
July and to hear words that would exalt American
independence and liberty to the skies, were bitterly
chagrined by his bold exposure of the crime of the
nation ; but nothing greater was seen on American
soil in the year 1852, neither anything more in keeping with the will of God. His friends and all anti-
slavery people were gratified by it ; it was an effort
which helped forward the good cause and brought
nearer the day of redemption.

George Lewis Ruffin, Judge of the district court of Charlestown, Mass., died in Boston in December 1887, leaving a widow and a four children. Fifty-two years before this he was born in Richmond, Virginia, of free parents. He was one of a family of twelve children, whose parents engaged a broken-down student at an enormous price to teach their children, with the result that at sixteen years of age George was not only well grounded in common English studies, but had some knowledge of Latin and the Classics and an excellent taste in English literature. At this time his mother, having decided that no effort which was for the ultimate good of her family was too great to be made, broke up her Southern home, came North with her brood and settled in Boston, where they might have every advantage possible. Here George attended the Chapman Hall School, and afterwards studied law at Harvard, and later in the office of Harvey Jewell, Esq. Before beginning the study of law, he began to earn his living as a barber, opening a shop on Green Street. While still a barber and only twenty-four years of age he married Josephine H. Pierre, a Boston girl, than in her sixteenth year. After his admission to the bar a good practice at once opened up to him.''

Mr. Ruffin began to represent the coloured people as a councilman, and was elected for three succes-

sive terms, and served on many of the most important committees.   Afterwards he went to the legislature for two successivè terms, and was never a
defeated candidate for any office.   He was appointed
Judge by Gov. Benjamin F. Butler in 1884. (?)

He was identified with many religious and charitable organizations, and all his life was a leading
spirit among the coloured people of Boston.

His widow, Josephine H. P. Ruffin, is one of the
picturesque figures of to-day.   Descended from a
pure-blooded English mother and a father who was
the result of the union of a N. E. Indian and
an African, fresh from his natives shores, she com-
bines the indomitable spirit and determination, the
courage and perseverance of those races.   She is an
active worker in the following organization :   The
Moral Education Society, The N. E. Women's
Press Club, The Woman's Charity Club and The
Massachusetts State Suffrage Association.   In 1891
she became editor of the Boston Courant, and after
that with her daughter started the Woman's Era, a
monthly paper devoted especially to the interest
of coloured women.   She was the originator of the
Woman's Era Club, an organization which numbers about 150 coloured women, and was one of the
pioneers in the Women's Club movement.   It was
Mrs. Ruffin through the Woman's Era, who was
instrumental in bringing about the first convention

of coloured women, from which has grown the large and promising organization known as the " National Association of Colored Women." She is now the recognized leader of the coloured women of Boston and is among the first in all public movements.

Phillis Wheatley, Frederick Douglass, Judge Ruffin and many others, graduates of Harvard, Yale, and Princeton, also graduates of grammar and high schools, whose names and doings we have no space, neither need, to notice, have shown what the ablest Negroes of the North can do, and their work is abundantly sustained by members of the race to-day. In medicine, law, education and art Negroes are working, and not a few have made efforts which have won universal commendation, and created for themselves spheres of activity and usefulness that are most satisfactory.

What of the Negro masses in the North? They may be found with the white masses, toiling together in peace. In foundries, dry-goods stores and markets; on passenger trains, freight trains, and in the parcel-express business; in hotels, private families and clubs; in barber shops, shoe-mending stores and meat stores; in every kind of human effort and wherever labour is put forth the Negro may be found taking a part, and earning his living in a manly fashion. Here his future is in his own hands, and we believe he will be guided by the spirit of God so to use his abundant opportunities that, throughout New England and in all Northern States, the remaining disinclination, which abides in the hearts of a minority, to admit him without reserve to every social privilege will pass away.

New England and Old England are much alike in many things, chiefest in this — love of liberty; and, from New England we expect an influence will yet go forth that will at least help win for the Negro in the South the advantages that are accorded him in the North.

HOME SCHOOL, BERTHOLD, NORTH DAKOTA.
SUSTAINED BY AMERICAN MISSIONARY ASSOCIATION.

CHAPTER X.

It is not possible to entertain just views and form a right estimate of the character of the Southern Negro, if it be forgotten that thirty years ago he was classed with hogs and treated by his owner with less kindness than he extended to his dogs. It must be remembered that he was in the power of his master; could own nothing; was bought and sold; and, as the horrible Dred Scott decision put it : — "he was supposed to have no rights which white men were bound to respect." White men could whip, starve, shoot and hang him without fear of legal interference, and in law he had no parents, no wife, no marriage, no human rights whatever. All this must be borne in mind when the Negro of the South is the subject under consideration.

They who know only the cities and towns of the South can not very easily form a correct idea of what is called "the black South," they are so unlike each other. In the "Black Belt," com-

prised in six Southern States, there are at least
four millions of Negroes, of whom not more than
half a million live in villages, towns and cities; the
other three and a half millions live on the plantations. This "Black Belt" has been called by one
who thoroughly understands it — "the vast black
malarial slough of the American Republic."

In Southern cities Negro life is not very different
from Negro life in the North; if any difference
obtain worth notice it is in greater wealth and finer
churches. In fact, Southern coloured churches and
congregations of the cities compare most favourably
with white churches and congregations, and, unfortunately, — this is a fault time and education
will correct — coloured people who form them are
not a little given to outward show and vanity.
They are quick, too, in emulation of the worst
features of "white society," and have already created an aristocracy of their own, which would be
amusing, if it were not reprehensible. These aris-
tocrats of the race refuse to recognize the name
Negro; call themselves *coloured* people; say that
Negroes are the "low blacks." In truth, they are
not Negroes,— are by blood much nearer the whites,
and could no doubt claim descent from the wealthy
slave-owners of the past. Some of them are almost
white, and have property, education and refinement. From this "aristocratic party" we hope

and expect much in the future, and shall be greatly
disappointed, their foolish pride and separation
from the blacks notwithstanding, if they do not
ultimately prove to be a power that will lift the
whole race of the South to a higher state of civilization.

Of all Southern cities Washington is called "the
coloured man's paradise," *the* city which accords
him a social standing, in which he enjoys life on
a higher plane. "The coloured aristocracy of
Washington," says the Buffalo Commercial, "numbers about four hundred all told. These Washington coloured swells live in fine houses. They are
possessed in many cases of large wealth. They
keep their own carriages, and they have servants
in abundance who minister to their wants. They
have everything, in short, that money and good
taste can suggest. . . . In their church worship the
coloured 'four hundred' are quite as exclusive as
their white neighbours, and a coloured day labourer
would hesitate as much to enter one of these sanctu-
aries as a white man of the same degree would in
presenting himself at the portals of Grace Church
in New York. There are other coloured churches
in Washington where the poor and fairly well-to-do
meet on equal terms, but they are not the churches
of the 'four hundred.' The swellest coloured
church in Washington is the Fifteenth Street Pres-

byterian. On Sunday mornings Fifteenth Street in the vicinity of the church is filled with carriages. In this respect they are aping the worst form of white snobbery." The Buffalo Commercial speaks truth, whose words we have quoted to afford the reader an idea not of this "swellest coloured church," but of those "other coloured churches where the poor and fairly well-to-do meet on equal terms." Such churches are found in many Southern cities, and what has been said of the Negro in the North may be applied to the Negro in the cities of the South, with differences arising out of state enactments, which do not affect him very seriously.

In the "Black Belt," where three and a half million Negroes live, everything is very different. In many parts of it the idea of a free church, independent of outside control, devoted to the task of teaching morality and education, is a thing almost unknown ; indeed a preacher who ventures to insist on cleanliness of life is looked upon with suspicion. Old superstitions survive, and even serpent worship is done, as in Africa, by some of the most ignorant. Among these millions of plantation Negroes necromancy and witchcraft, superstition and wild religious excitement, and a terrible divorce between faith and morals obtain, all which fearful things constitute the most awful judgment on the doings in past years of the "superior race" that this world has ever seen. " The superior race " has sown, and many yet sow, the wind, and are now gathering the whirl-wind, in which occupation they might be left without pity, if it were not for the thousands of christian men among them, who are innocent of the great crime of the past, and the millions of blacks who suffer, and are yet the subjects of a dense ignorance.

That two hundred and fifty years of slavery could end in anything better than ignorance, vice and crime no sane man might expect ; every heaven-illumined soul knows that virtue and self-control form no part of the heritage of human enthrallment. The chains of slavery are no longer worn in the South, it is true, but the chains of the Convict Lease System *are* worn, and inhumanity is yet prac-tised in the vilest manner, and vice and crime are *manufactured*. Under this infamous Convict Lease System the very worst features of slavery are re-tained and nourished. For offences which were scarcely noticed when he was a slave the Negro is sentenced to long terms of imprisonment, and then leased out to contractors, mining companies, and large plantation owners, who pay to the state forty cents a day for him. For larceny, sentences of fif-teen and twenty years have been given ; for hog steal-ing, twenty years ; for assault, two, five, six and seven years ; *and thousands of coloured men and women are serving out such sentences to-day, serving them out on plantations and in mines, making their lessees rich and gratifying the spirit of dominion which lives in the South.* In this " Black Belt " of the South, indeed in *every* Southern State, there is a determination to sustain " White Supremacy " at any cost of religion or humanity. A bishop of the Southern Methodist Church said recently : " Now-a-days, it seems the killing of Negroes is not so extraordinary an occurrence as to need explanation ; *it has become so common that it no longer surprises.* We read of such things as we read of fires that burn a cabin or a town. Unless the killing occurs in our own neighbourhood, we do not remember the names till the next morning." Comment on this statement were useless ; that a christian bishop can make it, and remain uncontradicted, reveals a condition of society than which none might be more horrible.

Some time in the year 1896 a very young boy wandered into the garden of General Flagles, of Washington, D. C., and innocently picked some grapes. He was a young Negro boy, a little fellow who had travelled out of his mother's sight, and knew not that he was doing any wrong. But the general's daughter, who watched him enter the garden, thought he did serious wrong, and, instead of warning the little fellow off, took a revolver and shot him dead on the spot. She was brought before

the authorities, pleaded guilty to a charge of invol-
untary manslaughter, and the sentence was — *three
hour's imprisonment* and a fine of *five hundred dollars.*
The fine was paid, the general's daughter spent
three hours in the sheriff's private parlour, and
"justice was done." The reader probably asks —
Can that be true? It is solemnly true; and these
pages could be filled many times with records of
cruelties and murders quite as heartless and diabolical. Lynching, shooting, burning and whipping of Negroes; convict plantation work, separation
of white and coloured children in school, and dis-
franchisement of voters by the thousand because
of colour; separate churches and railroad cars for
" Niggers ; " and, ignorance dense and awful are
the *common* things of the " Black Belt of the South,"
and at least three and a half millions of the Negro
race live in conditions, if not worse, little better than
those of slavery.

The Rev. Lyman Abbott, in a Sermon preached
before the American Missionary Assiociation at
Boston, in 1896, said : — " We do not object that a
Negro should be arrested, tried, convicted and executed for crime ; but we insist that he should be
arrested under law, tried under law, convicted
under law and executed under law. . . . The first
thing we demand in our redemptive process is law
working equal justice for black, for white, for red

and for yellow, and for any other colour that may appear. . . . In the second place, we demand for the inferior race equal industrial opportunities. . . . What we demand for the coloured man and for the Indian is that all doors shall be opened to him, all opportunities freely offered to him. The right and the liberty of industry given to him." . . . "The greater must serve the less. What does this mean ? It means, in the first place, just and equal rights before the law. . . . We protest against the heathen barbarism which hangs a white man for crime *after* trial and burns a black man for crime *without* trial." . . . "We claim for him — African and Indian — equal political rights. . . . The law which says to a *thrifty* Negro, 'You shall not vote,' and to a *thriftless* white, 'You may vote,' is an unjust and inequitable law." . . . "We stand too for this : . . . That they — African and Indian — shall have the same education and religious facilities and the same stimulus to intellectual and moral growth. Any scheme of education which proposes to furnish the Negro race only with manual and industrial education is a covert contrivance for *putting him in serfdom ;* it tacitly says that the Negro is the inferior of the white race, and therefore we will educate him so as to serve us."

Such words could not be spoken by any man, much less by Henry Ward Beecher's successor, if

just cause did not exist; if Negroes were enjoying
just and equal rights before the law, and equal
political rights, and receiving the education which
is given to Americans, — in the South, — it is perfectly clear they could *not* have been spoken. No
stronger proof of the contents of this book might
be given than this sermon of the Rev. Lyman
Abbott. It is known by every man in the country
that in the Southern States is a " vast black malarial
slough," a region of darkness and cruelty, vice and
ignorance, and it is equally well known that the
majority of whites in the South wish it to remain.
By intimidation and state enactment they *seek* to
keep the Negro ignorant and prevent him using the
ballot.

Men who have votes are always more powerful
and more respected than men without votes, as
every Englishman and American knows very well.
And the Negro knows it, too ; has been compelled
not only to know it, but understand it, by bitter
experience. The Southern States have in a great
measure disfranchised him, yet gain thirty-nine
votes in the electoral college by his presence in the
South ; that is, millions of Negroes are jockied out
of their political rights, and have no votes, but white
men go in their behalf to the electoral college and
help elect a President of the States. The case of
Mississippi will illustrate. Sixteen years ago there

were 130,278 coloured voters, who were in a majority
of 22,024 over the whites in that state; to-day, with
no material variation of proportions of population,
the whites have a majority of 60,000. How has it
been done? Simply by leaving the Negro off the
register. It is perhaps as near the truth as can be
when it is said that about one in every hundred
coloured men votes. This, as is easily seen, leaves
all executive power and the political and legisla-
tive machines in the hands of the whites, who fail
not to keep the Negro in that condition of poverty
and ignorance which is a notorious reflection on
everybody concerned.

Perhaps the reader asks — why does he not appeal? Why does he not *insist* on having his vote?
The answer is — this happens in the South, where
*he can choose between submission or punishment, —
lynching to death.* Some " Niggers " *are* allowed to
vote; it would never do to disfranchise the whole
race in the South; but they who are not put on the
register consult the comfort of their own skin by
" *keeping quiet.*"

The Negro of the cities of the South, then, may
be classed with the Negro of the North; but the
Negro of the " Black Belt," — the three or four millions who live on the plantations and in the woods
— cannot be classed at all. He is the disgrace of
America, the one solid, *indisputable proof* that, the

boasted civilization of the great United States notwithstanding, *all* Americans are *not* the most enlightened, neither the most humane. Millions of
white men may *call* themselves free, educated and
civilized, but when those same millions allow " Convict Lease Systems " and lynchings to obtain in
their midst without lifting hand to prevent them,
without sternly insisting that, state law or none,
they who lynch men to death are murderers and
must be punished, they must not be surprised if the
world think them drunk with lust of gold, blind with
the darkness of pride, and indifferent to righteous
government.

PLYMOUTH CHURCH. REV. HENRY WARD BEECHER SELLING A SLAVE.

CHAPTER XI.

The closing words of the last chapter are strong words, and would seem to cast an odious reflection on every Anglo-Saxon of the United States; the reflection, however, is only intended for those who are mentioned again and again in this book as the oppressors of the Negro. Other American citizens, of whom there are millions, must be spoken of in warmest words of gratitude, sincerest words of praise and highest words of commendation of which our speech is capable. They stand level with the noblest sons of God on earth, and, not only to the African, but to all needing help, instruction and civilization are ministers of grace. They are the salt of the great republic, and *will save it* in every highest sense, and banish from it the degrading facts of which this book treats. They are lovers of God and man; bright and intelligent; followers of the Christ and, like Him, generous; devoted to their country and ever jealous of its name and watchful for its future;

determined that it shall be just to all and the home of a common brotherhood.

In the dark days of slavery they deplored the huge evil that was in their midst, and did try, using all their power, to destroy it; and, since emancipation, have striven to bring to the emancipated their own high civilization. They have given millions of treasure, also time, thought and labour to the good cause, and not a few of them have spent their lives in "the Black Malarial Slough," surrendering comfort, home, even luxury, to go forth in the name of the Son of man to teach and christianize the ignorant and debased. Their work is like "the leaven which leaveneth the lump;" their lives are imperishable, whose influence abideth forever; their names are written in the hearts of men and women who thirsted for the water of kindness and hungered for the food of benevolence; heaven has received many of them into its rest and ordained them all to everlasting honour.

It is impossible to name them all; thousands of them will never be known for all they were worth and did excepting by "Our Father" who taketh note of both good and evil; but we must mention Arthur Tappan, William H. Seward, Charles T. Torrey, William Lloyd Garrison, Daniel Hand, Abraham Lincoln, John Brown, Rev. Henry Ward Beecher and Mrs. Harriet Beecher Stove. These

MR. BOOKER T. WASHINGTON, A. M.
PRINCIPAL OF TUSKEGEE NORMAL SCHOOL, ALABAMA.

have " cast " their " bread upon the waters," which
after many days is seen. We thank the Most
High for them and their labour, and with deepest
satisfaction and gratitude look upon the results of
the efforts they made.

Other friends of the Negro in the South are :
Rev. M. E. Streiby, D.D., Honorary Secretary of
the American Missionary Association ; The Pres-
byterian Board of Missions for Freedmen ; The
American Baptist Home Mission Society; The
Freedmen's Aid and Southern Educational Society ;
The Educational Society of the United Presbyterian
Church ; The Protestant Episcopal Commission ;
The African Methodist Episcopal Zion Church ;
The Coloured Evangelistic Fund — Southern Pres-
byterian Church ; The Coloured Baptist Church ;
and other similar institutions.   All these societies
and churches seek to uplift the millions of the
" Black Belt " and of other parts of the South by
imparting education and religion.

Another friend of the Negro in the South is
Booker T. Washington, himself an Afro-American ;
indeed he is a friend of the whole of the race to
which he belongs.   He is the founder of Tuskegee
Normal and Industrial Institute, situated in the
heart of the " Black Belt," Alabama, and is easy
of access to the great cotton plantations of Florida,
Mississippi, and Georgia.   Fourteen years ago he

started a school with thirty Negro children in a
building of no value; to-day he has not less than
five hundred students, several fine buildings, and
aboul fourteen hundred acres of land, which yields
wood, sugar cane, and grain. Too much praise
cannot be given to this school, and Booker T.
Washington is *beyond* praise. He has shown, as
Dr. Lyman Abbot said, that one Negro has ability,
and sends forth every year representatives of the
race to take a noble part in the common business
of life.

Of Guadalupe College, the Austin Daily Statesman says : — " One of the marvels of the times is
Guadalupe College at Seguin, Texas. It is a Negro
institution, owned, officered, managed, patronized
and supported by the Negroes themselves. It is a
grand and growing institution. The school is
organized with ten professors or teachers, and has
preparatory, scientific, collegiate, normal, theological and industrial departments. There are two
hundred and sixty-two pupils in the school, and
one hundred and seventy-one of these are boarding
in the institution, with six pupils in the senior class
for this year, and all doing good work. The young
men are taught carpentry, printing, farming, etc.,
and some of them make money to pay their way in
school in this way. The young women are taught
all kinds of domestic work, and one room is set aside

and provided with a number of sewing-machines where this skillful use is taught. They own a

GUADALUPE COLLEGE, SEGUINE, TEXAS.

printing-press and publish their own periodicals, and numbers of students learn the printers' trade. The character of the college is first rate in the town. All classes of white people testify to the order maintained on the school grounds, the moral character and the general behavior of the students, the high grade of work done in the school, and the culture and executive ability of the professors. Rev. D. Abner, Jr., President, is esteemed very highly as a scholar, gentleman and Christian. The college has a Bible department; also a theological class of young men preparing for the ministry, numbering some fifteen or twenty. This has been conducted by the president. The school is worthy of help and should have it.''

The Indianapolis Freeman says of Wilberforce University : — '' Wilberforce University was organized in 1856 by the M. E. Church. In its first board of twenty-four trustees was Hon. Salmon P. Chase, then Gov. of Ohio, and the fugitive slave's powerful advocate ; also Rev. Richard S. Rust and Bishop Daniel A. Payne. Its first active president was Dr. R. S. Rust, and its students were largely ' The natural children of Southern and South-Western planters.' While the war was still in progress, the future full of misgivings, without a dollar and alone, on the night of the tenth of March, 1863, Bishop Payne purchased the College property for $10,000. He at once associated with himself Rev. James A. Shorter, afterward Bishop, and Prof. J. G. Mitchell, now Dean of Payne Theological Seminary. An act of incorporation was duly taken out, with the broad principle embodied in it that ' There shall never be any distinction among the trustees, faculty or students on account of race, color or creed.' . . . Wilberforce University is consecrated to the christian enlightenment of the race. Over three hundred students are annually enrolled, the highest registrations in its history. Wilberforce will wield a power that shall be felt in the uplifting of the race from sea to sea.''

Howard University, Washington, D. C., Rev. J. E. Rankin, D. D., LL. D., President, also Professor

of Moral Philosopy and Christian Evidences, was
founded by Gen. O. O. Howard for all peoples
under the sun. It has among its pupils Asiatic, West
Indians, North American Indians, Anglo-Saxons
and Afro-Americans. It welcomes all such to-day.
It has seven distinct Departments under forty compe-
tent Professors and Instructors : Theological, Medi-

HOWARD UNIVERSITY, WASHINGTON, D. C.

cal, Legal, College, Preparatory, Normal and Industrial. This institution is always emphatically
Christian. Its Instructors believe in Christianity
as the only basis of true culture ; but pupils here
are given no denominational bias. The students
in all departments have aggregated six hundred and
twenty-nine ; the graduates ninety. This university

was organized under the auspices of the Government in 1867. It has never had a public or denominational constituency. It has none to-day. Only for aid funds — that is, for funds to assist indigent students and for the erection of needed buildings — has it ever made an appeal to the benevolent. It has taken its trustees and teachers from the ranks of all denominations while its aid funds have been distributed without regard to denomination. In the twenty-nine years of its existence it has graduated in all departments 1,354, of whom 1,253 are still living. Although the university is open to all races, yet those who have derived special advantage from it have been of African extraction. Five of the trustees are of the coloured race, and some of every one of its faculties of instruction. It is the only institution where the United States Government succeeds in providing equal facilities for a higher education of all classes of its citizens, without distinction of race or colour. Practically, and in large numbers, the Africo-American is not admitted to any of the Government schools in the land. It is so of all the other great schools of the nation. Is it too much to ask that the government shall do here for the coloured race what it is doing for the white race in other institutions such as West Point and Annapolis?

Among the evidences of Negro ability to establish and control great institutions, we have no better example than Livingstone College.   It was in the spring of 1882 that Bishops Hood and Lomax, with $3,000 of the $9,100 raised by Professor Price in England and $1,000 donated by the business men of Salisbury, purchased the site now occupied by Livingstone College.   The tract of land consisted of forty acres and the total cost of the place amounted to $4,600.   The Board of Bishops at the meeting in Chester, S. C., in September, 1882, adopted Zion Wesley Institute as a connectional school, electing Rev. J. C. Price, president, Rev. C. R. Harris, Prof. E. Moore, instructors, and Mrs. M. E. Harris as matron.   October 9, 1882, the Institute was opened on its own premises in Salisbury, and in 1886 or 1887 became Livingstone College, in honor of the great African explorer, David Livingstone.   The aim of the school has been to give a thorough literary training to coloured young men and women. The printing office is well equipped and much minute and pamphlet work has been done besides the publishing of the College Journal.   During the past five or six years the school has averaged an enrollment of over two hundred students, and has done its part in swelling the stream of workers for God and humanity.

The Hampton Normal and Agricultural Institute, at Hampton, Virginia, is situated on an arm of Chesapeake Bay, near the spot where Negro slaves

were first landed in 1619. Gen. Samuel Chapman
Armstrong, the enthusiastic young founder, understood the needs of the race. It was clear to him that
selected youths must receive training of hand, as
well as of head and heart, that they might go out
to teach and illustrate the dignity of labour and of
right living. It was also clear to him that nothing
should be given these young men and women except
the best possible opportunity of helping themselves,
and he was confident that the people of the country
would supply that opportunity. Beginning in 1868,
with two teachers and fifteen students in deserted
barracks, the school of 1897 requires fifty buildings
for the use and occupancy of its six hundred boarding pupils and eighty officers, teachers and assistants. The student pays for board ten dollars a
month in cash or labour. The school flies the flag
of no sect or party, but is religious in its influence.
About ninety per cent. of the nine hundred graduates
have engaged in teaching, and it is estimated that
over 150,000 pupils have been under their instruction. Among the graduates are some of the most
honoured men and women in the Southland, among
them, Booker T. Washington of Tuskegee.

The Grand Fountain of the United Order of True
Reformers is a fraternal beneficiary association,
organized under the laws of the State of Virginia,
and chartered in 1883. It was founded by an ex-

slave, Rev. W. W. Browne, in January, 1881. There were one hundred members in the organization, and the capital invested amounted to $150.   Its object then, was to take care of the sick, bury the dead, and to pay a death benefit to the widows and orphans of deceased members.   Since that time, it has increased its membership to more than thirty

GRAND FOUNTAIN ASSURANCE HEAD OFFICE,
RICHMOND, VA.

thousand.   Instead of one department, there have been established seven.   It has paid $287,924.25 in death benefits.   The organization owns property to the value of $100,000 and conducts the most successful Negro Bank in the country.   The savings bank was chartered by the Legislature of Virginia in 1888, and began operations in 1889.   It has the record of being the only bank in the city of Richmond that during the panic of 1893 did not at any time suspend the payment of specie. The business done by the bank up to date is nearly $3,000,000. The capital stock of the bank combined with that of the Order amounts to $135,000. The officers and members of this organization are all Negroes. There has been collected more than $4,000 toward the establishment of an Old Folk's Home for the aged and infirm members of the race. The Reformer, the official organ of the organization has a circulation of about 6,000 and is regarded as one of the best newspapers of the race. The President of the Organization is Rev. W. W. Browne; Cashier, R. T. Hill; Secretary, W. P. Burrell.

The American Missionary Association was established on the third of September, 1846. In the "Fiftieth Annual Report of the Executive Committee" we find that seventy schools, six colleges, two hundred and eighteen churches, and one hundred and twenty-seven ministers and missionaries are sustained by it, and that it has the care of 10,708 church members and 12,149 pupils, and that the amount expended during the year was $311,223.35 : about £62,604.5.7. Says this wonderful report : —
"Many who began in extreme humbleness are reaching into high places and are standing strong with their brethren of other races in the develop-

ment of superior powers." "In different localities in twelve Southern States, pupils numbering several thousands every year are taken through the intermediate, grammar, and normal courses of instruction, and graduates go out yearly to such work in life as they may be able to secure. Many avenues are closed to them which they are prepared to enter, and would enter if the *Ethiopian could change his skin*. As it is, the verdict of candour from observant Southern people comes to us that most of the pupils educated in our schools do honour to their instruction and to the principles which have been interwoven with their school life."

A friend of the Negro of the South is this American Missionary Association ; *the* friend *indeed* of the blinded white millions who despise the work that is done and oppress and lynch the Negro. Under the blessing of God this Association alone, unaided by any other human institution, is possessed of power to redeem the South in due time. Christ is in its midst, and " He must increase." To send thousands of educated, trained Negroes into the business of life every year, *to live among Negroes* and teach and preach, means something ; means more than any mortal can tell. Time is long and God is patient. The wickedness of man *must* be defeated and one grand human brotherhood *shall* be established. Schools, Colleges, Churches, almost three hundred of them, managed, financed, tutored and pastored by an Association depending on divine direction and inspiration, and many more by other christian agencies, and by Negroes themselves, cannot for ever be withstood ; their light and truth and love, borrowed from heaven, *must* and *will* illumine the darkest path, instruct the most ignorant mind, make warm and peaceful the coldest, saddest heart, and redeem the millions of the plantations and mines.

The Afro-American Newspapers, — such as The Indianapolis Freeman, The New York Age, The Coloured American, Washington, The Richmond Planet, The True Reformer, The Boston Courant and a number of other secular and denominational papers, — have done valiant work, and deserve the heartiest support of the race, whose interest they *do* boldly advocate. The names of Negro Ministers, who have attracted by patient well-doing and intelligent display of christian virtues the admiration of both white and black, are too numerous to mention ; but the late Rev. Theodore D. Miller, D. D., who was the beloved pastor of Cherry St. Baptist Church, Washington, Rev. William T. Dixon, D.D., Brooklyn, New York, Rev. Daniel W. Wisher, D. D., New York City, Rev. — Holmes, D. D., Richmond, Virginia, and Rev. G. W. Lee, D. D., Washington, may be spoken of as representative

men, and as leaders of the African people in America.
May they, and such as they, ever be found among
Christ's servants, doing the work of the Kingdom
of God.

It is impossible to conclude this chapter without
making a particular reference to the late Rev.
Henry Ward Beecher, who hated slavery and laboured to promote the Negro's interests.   Writing
of her husband, Mrs. Henry Ward Beecher says : —

"In 1847 Mr. Beecher became the pastor of Plymouth
Church, Brooklyn, and in his inaugural sermon he frankly
stated the position that he intended to hold in opposition to
human slavery. The majority of the church members agreed
with him, but the majority of the people of New York and
Brooklyn were Southern sympathizers. . . . He was abused
as a negro-worshiper; he was threatened with personal violence; a mob was formed in New York to tear down the
church in which he preached. . . . Amid these excitements
Mr. Beecher conceived the idea of giving to the people, who
now packed his church to hear him preach, an object-lesson
in Southern slavery, as he had seen it in Kentucky and as it
had been described to him by fugitives. . . . After a prelimi-
nary and very successful experiment in the New York Taber-
nacle, the first slave auction in Plymouth Church was held
on June 1, 1856. . . . That Sunday morning was a memorable
one. . . . When Mr. Beecher and I arrived at the church
entrance seemed impossible, and for fifteen or twenty minutes
several policemen were kept busy making a passageway for
us through the crowd so that we could reach the doors. The
church was densely crowded; every available foot of space
was occupied, and thousands were outside unable to gain
admission. When Mr. Beecher appeared on the platform a
deathlike stillness fell upon the entire auditorium. For a few
moments Mr. Beecher surveyed the wonderful assemblage
before him, and then, closing his eyes in prayer for a single

minute, he arose. . . . He began the service by reading the beautiful Scriptural story of the man who was cured of a withered hand, especially emphasizing Christ's question, 'Is it lawful to do good on the Sabbath Day or to do evil, to save life or to kill?' Then he said : 'About two weeks ago I had a letter from Washington, informing me that a young woman had been sold by her own father to be sent South — for what purpose you can imagine when you see her. She was bought by a slave-trader for twelve hundred dollars, and he has offered to give you the opportunity of purchasing her freedom. . . . Now, Sarah, come up here so that all may see you.'

The solemn, impressive silence of that vast Plymouth assemblage was absolutely painful as a young woman slowly ascended the stairs leading to the pulpit and sank into a chair by Mr. Beecher's side. Instantly assuming the look and manner of a slave auctioneer he called for bids. 'Look,' he exclaimed, 'at this marketable commodity — human flesh and blood, like yourselves. You see the white blood of her father in her regular features and high, thoughtful brow. Who bids? You will have to pay extra for that white blood, because it is supposed to give intelligence. Stand up, Sarah! Now, look at her trim figure and her wavy hair! — how much do you bid for them? She is sound in wind and limb — I'll warrant her! Who bids? Her feet and hands — hold them out, Sarah ! — are small and finely formed. What do you bid for her? . . . How much for her? Will you allow this praying woman to be sent back to Richmond to meet the fate for which her father sold her? If not, who bids? Come now! We are selling this woman, you know, and a fine specimen she is, too. Look at her. See for yourselves. Don't you want her? Now, then, pass the baskets and let us see.' . . . For a half hour money was heaped into the contribution boxes. Women took off their jewelry and put it in the baskets. Rings, bracelets, brooches piled one upon the other. Men unfastened their watches and handed them to the ushers. Above all the bustle and confusion of the remarkable scene Mr. Beecher's powerful voice rang out: 'Shall this woman go back to Richmond, or be free?' 'Free!' said several men, as they emptied their pockets into the collection baskets. . . . Just at this point, when the scene was becoming hysterical in its intensity, Mr. Louis Tappen rose and shouted above the din : 'Mr. Beecher, there need be no more anxiety as several gentlemen have agreed to make up the deficiency, no matter what it may be.' 'Then, Sarah, you are free!' cried Mr. Beecher, turning to the girl beside him. This statement inspired the almost frenzied audience to wildest demonstrations of enthusiasm, and quiet was not restored for several minutes until Mr. Beecher raised his hand for silence. Then in his usual, mellow voice he fervently exclaimed.: 'God bless Plymouth Church! I do not approve of unholy applause in the House of God ; but, when a good deed is well done, it cannot be wrong to give an outward expression to our joy.' . . .

Other slaves were sold by Mr. Beecher in Plymouth Church, and it is a proud record that not one had to be sent back to the slave-traders. 'I was glad by this means,' said Mr. Beecher, 'to arouse public feeling against the abomination of slavery, which I hate with an unutterable hatred.'

Mr. Beecher was often summoned to Washington by President Lincoln and by Secretary Stanton for consultation upon public affairs, his advice being prized as disinterested and without political bias. Whenever he called at the White House his persistent appeal to President Lincoln was, 'Free the slaves! Free the slaves!' 'There is no law,' replied Lincoln, 'by which I can abolish slavery, except as a military necessity.' 'Do you promise,' he pressed, 'that you will issue a proclamation of emancipation if ever the military necessity shall occur?' 'Certainly,' replied Lincoln, 'with all my heart.'

One morning, at our home in Brooklyn after he had read the newspaper reports of military affairs, Mr. Beecher was strongly agitated. 'I think that I shall go to Washington,' he said, and gave the usual instructions about the prayer-meeting and the correspondence. I am told that he went to the Fulton Ferry, and crossed and re-crossed several times, as if undecided as to what course to pursue. At length he seemed to arrive at the conclusion that steam could not carry him to Washington fast enough for his purpose. So he entered the nearest telegraph office and sent this message to the Presi-

dent: 'Is there not a military necessity now? Will you keep
your promise?' Then he returned home and busied himself
with church affairs. As the hours passed he became more
preoccupied and absorbed, speaking to no one and answering
no question until it had been twice or thrice repeated. When
we sat down to dinner he pushed his plate away untasted. The
doorbell rang and a telegram was brought to him. As he
opened the envelope, his hand trembled visibly. The message
consisted of only two words, but they meant the freedom of a
race. They were: "Yes! LINCOLN.' It is a sweet thought
that connects the freedom sales of Sarah and Pinky, in Plymouth Church, with the emancipation of the colored people,
and that gives to Mr. Beecher, who had labored so long, so
zealously and so eloquently for abolition, the honor of receiving the first intimation from President Lincoln of that proclamation which has shed upon this country even a greater glory
than the Declaration of Independence.''

There is hope for the Black South. But probably the reader asks — is it *really* true that, in the
presence of all this christian life and labour, Negroes are down-trodden, treated with cruelty, and
lynched to death? It is most sadly true. And it
is true that all this christian effort is put forth in
behalf of about four millions of Negroes, born
slaves and children of slaves, — not much different
from slaves now — who know little of all the precious knowledge this world contains, and have less
of its civilization. But "the night is far spent."
In a little while the morning of hope and promise of
future good will spread its light over the " Black
South," and will kiss into newness of life the Afro-
-American people, and the great republic will be
cleansed of its deepest stain of sin.

OPEN AIR KINDERGARTEN. LISTENING TO THE BIRDS.
SUSTAINED BY AMERICAN MISSIONARY ASSOCIATION.

CHAPTER XII.

CONCLUSION.

A few closing observations must be made. We desire, however, no longer to dwell on this Negro tragedy; but to make the following suggestions.

First, we suggest that Christian people use every opportunity of creating a Christian public opinion on this Negro question. Let not any think that the opinion of England, France, Germany and other European countries counts for nothing in the United States. Americans are proud of their country, and boast of its liberty and equality, and are quick to feel the touch of foreign reproach. If foreign ministers of religion preached with one accord on the barbarity of Negro treatment in the Southern States of America, and if resolutions were passed in condemnation thereof, and if sermons and resolutions were published in American papers, or distributed over the country in pamphlet form, thousands of citizens who now leave the work of amelioration to the best men of North and South would be moved, if only to gratify feelings of national pride, to help establish majesty of law, and so end these barbarities. Let none think that Christian Americans would resent such work as interference; if any were to object they would not be Christians. All Christ's

men will welcome gladly and gratefully the influence of such work as a gift from God, and will be
made stronger to discharge successfully the divine
duties they have undertaken.

Second, we suggest that prayer be made for the
"Black Malarial Slough" of the United States.
Christian education, Christian sympathy, and the
love of the Christ are *the necessity* of the Negro race
in the "Black Belt." Prayer offered before the
Throne of Mercy in faith *must reach* Christ's servants
who toil among the black millions that have inherited ignorance and debasement, and can only result
in enlargement of their wisdom and spiritual power;
using which they shall more certainly and rapidly
extend the kingdom of the Saviour. "Ask and ye
shall receive; seek and ye shall find; knock and the
door shall be opened unto you." Think of Negro
men, women and children as the subjects of greatest
hardship, blackest vice and foulest cruelty, and let
prayer go up to God for the "Black Belt" of the
Southern States of America.

With undying sympathy for the coloured race,
and gratitude for all good men who have toiled,
given of their substance, and died to educate and
christianize Negroes, and in the hope, which is born
of faith in "Our Father," that barbarity and cruelty
may in due time pass from this world, the writer
concludes this effort of love.

APPENDIX.

THE GEORGIA CONVICTS.

A COLORED CRITIC ON THE APOLOGY FOR THE LEASE SYSTEM.

To the Editor of the Transcript:—

Your correspondent at Atlanta, Ga , made some interesting statements in his communication of the 4th inst. concerning the future management of convicts in that State, and also about the origin of the convict lease system of Georgia and the outdoor work for colored convicts, all of which merit particular consideration.

The writer says that " a great reform has been brought about under the new law," which is not entirely true, as that law has not gone into effect as yet.   He very probably meant a great reform has been proposed by the commission appointed by the good governor of Georgia the latter part of last year.   If the changes recommended by the commission are put into effect, humanity will win in a large measure ; viz., through the separation of the sexes and the removal of the juvenile convicts from daily association with hardened criminals.   Such would be a great step in advance of the old system, and one which will meet with the ready approval of all lovers of humanity and all those interested in the advancement of society.

It is earnestly hoped that one reform after another may continue, until the present barbarous methods of dealing with convicts in the South are absolutely abolished.

As to the true origin of "The Convict Lease System" of Georgia, it is entirely true, and the State records will bear out the fact that the lease system of managing State convicts was

enacted by statute law in that State in 1869, just three years after
the right of franchise had been conferred upon the freedmen of
the South

As your correspondent states, it is very probable that General
Thomas H. Ruger of the United States Army, acting military
governor of Georgia in 1868, did lease convicts to the highest
bidder; and in that same year Governor Bullock, the only Republican governor of Georgia, may have, and doubtless did, hire
out convicts without the consent of the people of Georgia.

But the mean case in point here is this : The true origin of
the old lease system of Georgia, which has brought reproach
upon the good name of that State, and which has also justly
merited condemnation from right-thinking people in Georgia
and elsewhere.   The facts in the case show that in 1869 a Democratic committee of a Democratic House originated the law,
which was supported by both parties in the Senate and approved
by a Republican governor.   Hence the responsibility belongs to
Republicans and Democrats.

Poverty of the State was the flagrant excuse for enacting such
a measure.   Instead of reducing the taxpayers' burdens, as the
law was supposed to do, they have been increased each succeeding year to pay judges, juries, and tremendous jail fees.   With
the process of time under the lease system in vogue in the Southern States, the rich grow richer and the poor poorer, for only
the rich men are lessees.

After stating that the cause for the convict lease system was
the poverty of the State, your correspondent goes on and says
that "Democratic legislatures, for the same reasons, continued
the system under restraints which reduced its bad features to a
minimum, postponing to a later and more prosperous period the
permanent solution of the penitentiary problem."

In reply to such a statement it is evident from every report
that has been made by investigating committees since May 5,
1870, looking to a better condition of affairs in the prisons of
Georgia, that the prisoners in the State have suffered in a manner beyond human belief.

From the report of an investigating committee which met in
Atlanta, May 5, 1870, it is seen that John Darnell, principal
keeper of the State penitentiary, was examined, and acknowl-

edged that great suffering and punishment were known to prevail in some of the convict camps. Public opinion was aroused, and for a time certain reforms were anticipated. No change was made in the management of convicts other than an increased number of contractors, and the convicts were scattered all over the State.

In 1874 His Excellency the Governor favored a longer lease, and the following is an extract from his message to the Legislature that year :—

"The number of convicts is increased to 664 : 90 are white, 574 are colored persons; 1 white, 19 colored women. I would suggest a longer lease term than two years. The profitable employment of so large a force would involve a heavy outlay on the part of the contractors. Of the convicts in the penitentiary five to one are colored persons, most if not all of whom, by reasons of their ignorance and former habits of life, can never be profitably employed in any of the mechanical arts."

In 1887 a Democratic United States Senator from Georgia, while representing his State in the national Capitol at Washington, was working 525 convicts in coal mines, in iron foundries and around coke ovens. In the same year the executive of Georgia (a Democrat) was a lessee answerable to the State in a bond of $37,500 for convict labor. Said bond is lawful until April, 1899. The official records for 1887 in the governor's department show who were contractors for convict labor at that time.

The Georgia Penitentiary Company, No. 1. Joseph E. Brown (United States Senator), Julius Brown, W. D. Grant & Co., and Jacob Seaver, Boston, Mass.

The Georgia Penitentiary Company, No. 2. B. G. Lockett, L. A. Jordan, W. B. Lowe and John B. Gordon (governor).

The Georgia Penitentiary Company, No. 3. Thomas Alexander, W. D. Grant, W. W. Simpson, J. W. Murphy (clerk in State treasury), and W. H. Howell.

During the time these gentlemen were lessees the State's contract called for $25,000, but the State's treasurer's report fails to show that that amount or anywhere near it was realized. R. A. Alston, chairman of an investigating committee, in an open

letter to the *Atlanta Constitution*, December, 1878, exposed the
evils practiced in the convict camps, for which he was killed by
a sub-lessee in the State capital March 11, 1879. It must be remembered that all such devilish action was carried on under
Democratic administration, though no one will deny but that
the Republicans and Populists are just as miserable sinners as
the Democrats of Georgia. Every bill that has been presented
to the Legislature of Georgia during the past twenty-eight years
praying for a reform of the prison system in that State, has been
strenuously opposed and defeated by the Democrats. The measure which passed the Legislature of Georgia last year was
whipped through on strict party lines. It was done to prevent
showing Democratic incompetency, and not through a desire to
bring about any particular reform of the lease system.

Republicans and Populists alike voted against the measure, so
as to defeat it with the hope that the people of Georgia would
rebuke the Democrats at the next election for failing to carry
out their will.

It is absurd to say that convicts in Georgia have been hu-
manely treated. The investigation inaugurated by Governor
Atkinson last year revealed the fact that convicts in that State
had been treated in the most brutal manner. The treatment of
women in convict camps was too shocking for public print.
The death rate among the prisoners was enormous,—one out of
every four; which was due to poor food, lack of clothes, sleeping
on the bare ground, and the terrible punishment inflicted by the
brutal guards. There is no comparison to be made between the
death rate of the convicts and that of the colored race outside
the prison walls in the State of Georgia.

The statement that " one fourth of the convicts of Georgia
came from Atlanta, Savannah and Macon, where the negroes occupy the slums and are victims of want, disease and crime," is
simply to play upon the fancy of the readers, and cause them to
think that there is no remedy other than the lease system to
check crime among the negroes.

The fact is, the lease system in vogue in the Southern States
is a true relic of slavery with ten times the severity of the old
system, and it operates upon the colored race with particular de-
moralizing effect. It is interesting to know that of the 2,235

convicts in Georgia, 2,038 are negroes, while only 197 are white, when in that State the white inhabitants outnumber the blacks by far. There are people charitable enough to say that criminality of the blacks is the cause for such remarkable disparity of white and colored criminals in Georgia and in other Southern States, which is by no means true. I have been in Southern courts, and have seen colored men, women, and youths convicted and given long and hard sentences for the most frivolous offences, for which a white person would not even be arrested.

It is very strange that indoor work punishes black convicts in Georgia more than it does black convicts in Massachusetts. I made a visit to the Reformatory at Concord last May, and addressed the boys in that magnificent institution. Upon particular inquiry concerning colored boys, I was informed by the authorities, noble-hearted Christian gentlemen, that colored boys had made pretty good records; no worse than the average white boy, to say the least. No mention was made that they had been invalids, because of working inside with the white boys. The truth of the matter is this: Massachusetts is endeavoring to reform the unfortunate, while Georgia is realizing a revenue wrung from the muscles of her convicts. During slavery the slaves were worked for the most part in the open air, and the same is true in regard to colored convicts.

Too much praise cannot be given to Governor Atkinson and those who have joined him in his endeavor to bring about a better condition for the convicts in Georgia.

From the best intelligence that can be had from the colored population of Georgia, Governor Atkinson will receive the colored vote as often as he is nominated for governor of that State. He is more just to the colored people than any governor Georgia has had since emancipation.   D. E. TOBIAS.

BOSTON.

THE PROGRESS OF CIVILIZATION IN KANSAS.

IN DEFENSE OF THE NEGRO.

White Women on Lonely Plantations Surrounded by Blacks and in No Danger.—Kindly relations Between the Two Races.—Some Causes of the Recent Troubles.

A Southern woman whose family is the one white family on a cotton plantation in lower South Carolina, a tract embracing 5,000 acres and peopled with colored tenants numbering thirty-five families in all, maintains that the negro is as chivalrous and kindly by nature as the white man, and that the assumption that his presence is a menace to the white women of the South is most unfair. In speaking of recent disturbances in the South and the comments and statements which they have provoked, she said :—

" I and my girl friends, young women who happened to be visiting us, habitually walked and rode and drove everywhere on that plantation and in the surrounding country, in out-of-the-way lonely roads and woods tracts, wherever we happened to want to go. We never met with anything but respectful and kindly treatment, and the men of the family never seemed to apprehend that we would be in danger. The negro has as much chivalry and courtesy in mind for the native Southern woman or for any white woman as a white man has, and is willing and ready to do her service on the slightest intimation that she needs such.

" And another thing. The negroes living on this particular plantation were not immaculate, and at times there were strained relations between them and the landowner or employer; but they never visited this disaffection on the landowner's women folks, who trusted them. Sometimes a bale or a couple of bales of cotton would be taken from the yard or the ginhouse at night. The negroes would help the sheriff to track the bale and to detect the thief, and he would be sent to the penitentiary. Invariably when that negro had served his term he came back to his old haunts and went to work again. If he harbored resentment it never showed itself in brutality. The lumber mill on the place was burned down twice, two years apart; the smokuhouse was robbed, the potato banks and sugar-cane banks were opened, and there were other depredations, showing that the tenants were not altogether saintly; but their slips and back-slidings never took the form of insult or outrage. I have read of lynchings and of the need for them, but in each case with the feeling that there was another underlying cause,—some harsh, browbeating treatment of the negro that culminated, even if indirectly, in this form of outrage. I doubt seriously if a true-born Southern lady, one whom the negroes respected as such, was ever subjected to rude treatment by a negro tenant or employee. And the unfortunate woman victim of lynching events will, in nearly every case, be found to be associated with the common, underbred, negro-hating order of white men in the Southern white population; people whose fathers never owned slaves or owned much of anything, mentally or materially, and who are jealous of the negro's advancement and fitness for places of trust.

"I have a friend, a Southern woman, barely twenty-eight years old and of attractive personality, who at this moment is living on the little remnant of her father's estate, with only an aged maiden aunt for companion, in a homestead entirely surrounded by negro cabins. The nearby plantations have been sold to cotton factors and storekeepers, who have turned them over to an agent to be rented out in little lots to negroes, practically putting the girl's home in a black belt. This white woman has only the kindliest relations with her negro neighbors. When she drives off to the town, ten miles away, to buy supplies, they get her to execute little commissions that will save them the journey. In return the black men farmers, the sons of the men who once worked on the old family acres, give practical advice to 'Miss Lou' as to what sort of seed will go best in certain plots of ground, how the young girl farmer can best and most economically feed her stock, and other points, tips that experience has taught them and that are valuable. Let the statement of Mrs. Felton, or whatever Georgia woman is crying out against the negro and attributing innate brutality to him, be repeated in this girl's presence, and it would be received with scorn and incredulity.

"'I'm not afraid,' she would say. 'They would never harm me.'

"Another thing. How comes it that the negro nature is so brutal and debased now, when all during the civil war he nobly carried out the trust of protecting and advising the white women and children that were left in his care? All the able-bodied white men, every able-bodied and half able-bodied white boy in the Southern country, were away at the front, and their wives and sisters and sweethearts were entirely at the mercy of the negro men. Sometimes hundreds of negro men and boys were on a single plantation where only the mistress and her daughters, and maybe three or four women relatives—refugees from a bombarded seaport—were installed. There was never any hint of a need for lynching then, and the negro's nature cannot have changed so radically in a little more than one generation.

"The old order of planter obtains in the South still—the man who is stung to the quick by injury done his black friends, and who has a kindly feeling for them as he has for any hapless irresponsibles. The old Colonel by courtesy, too steeped in prejudice and tradition to admit that the negro has mental aptitude, is yet for that very reason kinder to him than the man who regards him as altogether an equal and is on the watch to work him and make whatever can be made out of him. The old idea, ' I must look out for my women and niggers,' has something of a hold yet in the old school mind, and the negro freedman knows that the white person of the right sort, rich or poor, would scorn to take advantage of an inferior. The old order of planter did not want his slave property taken away from him, and does not now want to see the negro hold office; but, in a material way, he is the black man's friend, and the black man knows it well. As for the sons of these old school people, they are as indignant as anybody when harsh usage is dealt out to the negro. Hasn't the white man been side by side with the negro and had him for constant attendant and companion ever since both were babies and their grandfathers were babies? And don't they hunt with him now, by accident if not by prearrangement, every autumn season, sharing in common the man-to-man primeval enjoyments of the forest and field? How can there be a serious race issue between people joined in such bonds, having one common country and interests?

"'Jake Isham been took up, sir, and he say could you come
down and git him out,' is a common plaint at the harvest season
in South Carolina, when all the Jakes and Sams and Sambos go
to town and indulge in poor whiskey and get into scrapes. And
the white man, who remembers Jake as a self-appointed body-
guard ever since the two could toddle (with Jake always the
taller and stronger for his age), does not inquire what Jake has
done to be 'took up' for, but harnesses up and goes to the
rescue.

"The negro at the South just now has three distinct elements
pulling at him and getting him upset and askew. First the
shopkeepers, who have no qualms of conscience as to the advisa-
bility of getting all they can out of the unsophisticated negro
population. The blacks come in constant and direct touch with
this class, and they are white people, even if they do not tend to
elevate the white race in the estimation of the black man. The
unteachable and illiterate grade of 'poor buckra' is another
and a signal factor in the negro's undoing. Men of this class
seldom have negroes working for them, but come in touch with
the negro in public places and at common resorts, and wrangle
with them and make them feel that a stigma attaches to their
color. The unscrupulous and fanatical white radicals and the
educated negro leaders, who are to be forgiven for errors in tact
and doing, are a third source of disquietude to the negro who
would like to be left in peace to work and make something of a
home for himself independent of politics and political issues.
Among them all, the poor, kindly natured, ill-equipped black
man has a sorry time of it trying to reconcile odds and problems
that even great understanding cannot cope with. Only one
thing the normal, work-a-day negro is sure of, and that is that
his old white people and their kind are his friends, will look
after him when he is sick, help him out of serious trouble, and
give illuminating glimpses into matters of law and business that
help smooth out the wrinkles on his brow.

"'I had just step in dis mornin' to ask if you will look in de
book and tell me how old I is,' a stalwart black fieldworker,
farming on his own hook, will ask of his father's former owner
some dreary winter morning; and then the old slave register or
ledger will be got down from the shelf, and the white man care-

fully scans its pages to where the birth entry of this Violet Handy's fourteenth child was listed fully forty-five years ago. The age question settled, the farmer stays a moment to talk over prices and proceeds and get information as to public events,— information that he will rehearse word for word to his colored visitors for days to come.

"Another day toward Christmas, maybe, the black farmer's wife appears soliciting a private interview with the white farmer's wife or sister. Taken into a private room where nobody will be likely to intrude, it turns out that she wants to learn the exact denomination of the bill she is to take with her to town to invest in shopping.

"'Is this $5 or $2 or what, Miss Julia?' she asks diffidently, producing the paper bill in question. 'My ole man say it's a five, but I ain't know for certain, and I want you to 'lowance just how much I ought to pay out for a black alpaca apon and two head handkerchief and a cloak for Martha's baby. I ain't trust them town store people. When you take things out in trade they cheat you, and it's worse when you pay cash down.'

"On this the white woman writes an order, stipulating price and quality of articles for her black friend, and the storekeeper gives the woman the proper attention and the correct amount of change.

"As long as there are primitive intimate dependencies like these between the races the white women are safe from negro insult. In critical times of sickness and sadness the negroes are first of all in their sympathy for the white people, and only a couple of years ago, when a gentle-minded planter was about to be borne to his last resting place and the white pallbearers stood at hand to perform the task, six of the black retainers and servitors of the place appeared in the hall, each combed and dressed in such fit garb as he could muster, and one, the miller, stepped up bashfully to the planter's son and asked to be allowed to carry the old boss out of the house. In the cities the negroes are tempted into mischief through lack of occupation, and among the half-educated and turbulent white and black element, riots may occur, but the real backbone of the Southern country has regard for its black people and would see them get ahead. A serious schism between the races is out of the question; there

THE NEGRO DISFRANCHISED

THE FIRST STEP INTO A NEW SLAVERY

SENATOR TILLMAN IN CONGRESS—"We do our best to keep every negro in our State from voting"

are too many ties to bind them together, and whatever report to
the contrary, the people who have studied the negro and know
him best will maintain that he is kindly and straightforward and
tender-hearted, the reverse of the brute that he is portrayed.
He loves peace and sunshine and rhythm, and would far rather
be docile and pleasant than sulky. He is easily led, and that is
the chief stumbling block. There are so many trying to lead
him, and most of these, with the exception of such as Booker
Washington, are trying to lead him to their own advantage."

IS THE NEGRO A MAN?

THE REV. DR. BRUNDAGE STANDS FOR SOCIAL AS WELL AS POLITICAL EQUALITY.

The Rev. Dr. William M. Brundage, pastor of the First Unitarian Church, preached last night on the topic: "Is the Negro
a Man?" Protesting against the wrongs that have been done
the negro, the Rev. Dr. Brundage spoke as follows :—

"In the year 1833 John C. Calhoun, United States Senator
from South Carolina, is reported to have said 'that if he could
find a negro who knew the Greek syntax, he would then believe
that the negro was a human being and should be treated as a
man.'

"How was the negro to learn his a, b, c's, to say nothing of
Greek syntax, when in the state of South Carolina it was considered a crime to teach him? As early as 1740 the colony of
South Carolina enacted this law: 'Whereas, the having slaves
taught to write, or suffering them to be employed in writing,
may be attended with great inconvenience: Be it enacted, That
all and every person or persons whatsoever who shall hereafter
teach or cause any slave or slaves to be taught to write, every
such person or persons shall forever for every such offense for-
feit the sum of £100 current money.'

"Very soon it was forbidden to teach a slave to read as well
as to write. For two hundred and forty-five years, from the
landing of the first slaves at Jamestown, Va., in 1619, to the
Emancipation Proclamation of Abraham Lincoln in 1863, the
negro in America was treated as a beast of burden, 'a hewer of

wood and a drawer of water," a mere instrument of production, a slave. In Africa he was cruelly hunted as cattle, and when captured, thrust like cattle into the hold of a ship and brought to America to be sold to the highest bidder. Holland, English and Spanish ships alike were engaged in this horrible slave trade. Indeed, for thirty years, from 1713 to 1743, the Englishmen controlled the slave trade as a monopoly.

"During the entire period of negro slavery his Christian master studiously sought to keep the slave as a docile brute, to repress his growing intelligence, to crush out every dawning aspiration. Christian ministers, like Bishop Meade of Virginia, thus instructed him : ' Almighty God hath seen pleased to make you slaves here, and to give you nothing but labor and poverty in this world, which you are obliged to submit to, as it is his will that it should be so. Your bodies, you know, are not your own; they are at the disposal of those you belong to,' etc. 'When correction is given you, you either deserve it or you do not deserve it. But whether you really deserve it or not, it is your duty, and Almighty God requires that you bear it patiently.'

"By such instruction as this the negro slave was kept in the condition of proper servility. Compare the condition of a negro slave in Mohammedan countries with his condition in Christian America. The slave who becomes a Mohammedan that moment becomes a free man. No social bar separates him from his fellow Mohammedans. In Christian America when the slave became a Christian he became a more docile slave, that was all ; for did not the Almighty God ordain that the white man should be his lord and master? To claim that brotherly treatment was due him from his fellow Christian believers was a sin. To defend himself against the cruelty and outrage of the white man was a crime.

"'Put out the light, and then, put out the light,' was the maxim of the slaveholder in every age. And the light of intelligence was put out and kept extinguished for centuries. In the year 1863 the negro slave was emancipated by the proclamation of Abraham Lincoln. The Thirteenth Amendment to the Constitution of the United States, ratified in 1865, forever prohibited slavery in the United States. The Fourteenth Amendment made all freedmen citizens of the United States, while the Fifteenth

Amendment, ratified in 1870, gave the ballot to the freedmen and secured to them the use of it. Thus, as far as the law could do it, the negro had become a man and a citizen.

"A generation has come and gone since then, and yet I come to you in all seriousness to-night with this question: Is the negro a man, to be respected and treated as a fellow man? In the eyes of the law he has been a man for thirty-seven years. In the judgment of all thoughtful, unprejudiced students of society he has played the part of a man. After centuries of cruel repression, during which every possible effort was made to break his spirit, to crush out his manhood, to darken his intelligence, within a single generation he has made greater progress than most people have made within several generations, and that, too, in the face of the bitterest opposition. During a single generation he has decreased illiteracy among his people more than 30 per cent. During a single generation he has accumulated nearly a billion of dollars' worth of property, including homes for 400,000 negro families. He has honorably entered all the professions. He has become poet and painter of distinction; young negro men and women graduates of colleges and higher educational institutions.

"Nineteen hundred years ago the ancestors of the Anglo-Saxon race were rude barbarians in the forests of Northern Europe, offering human sacrifices in the worship of their gods. Two hundred and fifty years ago the ancestors of Paul Laurence Dunbar, Dr. Edward W. Blyden, Henry O. Tanner, Dr. W. H. Councill, Booker T. Washington and Rev. P. Thomas Stanford, A.M., M.D., D.D., LL.D., were naked savages in the jungles of Africa.

"Our Anglo-Saxon ancestors were never stolen from their homes and subjected to brutal slavery as were the ancestors of these men. What little civilization we possess to-day is the product of the labors of more than fifty generations, while these distinguished negroes, children of slaves, are emulating us on our own fields with our own weapons.

"A correspondent in the New York *Times* a few weeks ago described an amateur performance of modern opera by negro young men and women of Washington, and he declared that he had never before seen such refined and intelligent acting by amateurs, and these cultured ladies and gentlemen were, for the most part, children of slaves.

"And yet, in the face of all these facts, and multitudes of others that might be cited, I ask in all seriousness, Is the negro a man? How many of our American white people, even in the North, actually consider him to be a man, a fellow man, and treat him as a man? Politicians are glad enough to get his vote. He is good enough to work in our kitchens, to prepare our food, to wait upon us at the table, to care for our children, to black our shoes, to drive our carriages, to act as porter in Pullman sleeping cars, to run errands for us. But to be our friends and equals, to sit beside us in our churches and lodge rooms, to work beside us in shop and store, to be fellow guests at hotels, to be invited at our homes, to live beside us on the street—that is a very different matter. Here the wretched caste spirit dominates us. The negro is not a man, an equal; he is an inferior being, to pity and patronize, it may be, but to secretly despise.

"Listen to these words of Edward A. Freeman, the historian, in describing his visit to the United States in 1882: 'The law may declare the negro to be the equal of the white man; it cannot make him his equal. To the old question, Am I not a man and a brother? I venture to answer, No. The negro may be a man and a brother in some secondary sense; he is not a man and a brother in the full sense in which every Western Aryan is a man and a brother.'

"Edward A. Freeman simply speaks out frankly what multitudes of white people secretly think and feel.

"A negro in our city, a high-minded, cultured gentleman, whose wife is a refined woman, a true lady, has found it almost impossible to secure a respectable home in Albany. Real estate agents will not and cannot rent him a house anywhere except in the poorer quarters of the city. He can live in the neighborhood of the houses of prostitution, in the tenderloin district or in the crowded business quarter, but not on our respectable streets. The real estate agents but represent the property owners for whom they act and the white public whom they serve. This is not a supposititious case; it represents the actual condition of caste in the city of Albany to-day. The negro, no matter what his cleanliness, culture and refinement may be, no matter what may be his excellences of character, is not a man, is not fully and freely accorded the rights and privileges of a man. Although he may be a white man's peer in every respect, intellectually and morally, yet because of the color of his skin he is the white man's inferior and is made to feel his inferiority in a great variety of ways.

"With all our boasted civilization, in the face of all the claims we advance for America as the land of the free, a refuge for the oppressed, there is no place in our country to-day where a negro baby is not handicapped in the struggle for life by the mere fact that he is a negro child. Because we white men have wronged the negro, therefore we hate and despise him. Because we Christians by superior force made him a slave, therefore we consider him our inferior. Although we broke his chains and bade him go free, we have not yet begun to make full and complete reparation for the hideous wrong of the past; we have not yet begun to recognize him as a fellow man and to treat him as a man.

"The self-respecting negro no longer pleads for our pity or for alms at our hands; what he claims as his right is justice, liberty, fair play, social equality. What he justly insists upon to-day is that mere color of skin shall be no bar to social and industrial advancement. He asks for no special privileges; all that he asks is that he shall be treated as a man, respected as a man. Who can deny the justice and reasonableness of his claim.

"Thus far I have but called your attention to the social ostracism of the negro in our Northern communities. I have a still darker picture to lay before you when I describe the negro's condition in the South.

"No man loves peace and harmony more ardently than do I, but I must confess that when I read in our Northern newspapers to-day all the honeyed words of compliment and conciliation bestowed upon the Confederate soldiers who fought to preserve the institution of slavery and who persist in denying to the negro his rights as a citizen and a man, I believe that I feel something of the indignation which the negro himself must feel. We cry, ' Peace, peace, when there is no peace.' I would that every one of you might read an article in the *Nineteenth Century* for last December entitled, ' A Negro on the Position of the Negro in America.' Facts are given in that article which seem incredible. Until I verified most of these facts by an appeal to other witnesses I could not believe that conditions were as bad as therein described. A distinguished Southern writer, George W. Cable, because he has dared to tell the truth concerning his own people, has been practically exiled to the North, has published a book entitled, *The Silent South*, which establishes the main position of the negro writer in the *Nineteenth Century*.

" We are all more or less well informed concerning the lynchings of negroes in the South, but few of us appreciate the extent of these outrages. During the year 1899 more than 100 negroes, six of whom were women, were lynched without the semblance of a trial on the following charges: 'self-defense, race prejudice, stock-poisoning, talking too much, murder, larceny, barn-burning, suspected robbery, writing an insulting letter to a white man, horse-stealing, incendiarism, attempted murder, malpractice, for suppressing evidence in court, for giving evidence in court, rioting, etc.'

" Booker T. Washington, of Tuskegee, stated one year ago that during the past six years, from 1893 to 1899, 900 negroes had been lynched. We are told that negroes are lynched for 'unspeakable crimes'; they are lynched for any crime and for no crime at all, but for the mere suspicion of it.

" Samuel Creed Cross, of West Virginia, a white man, gives the following instances which came under his own observation: ' At McDonough, La , a negro was lynched for attempting to rob a store. In South Carolina another negro was ferociously mobbed and lynched for stealing an old worthless mule. Another for breaking a labor contract was viciously lynched and whipped to death with a buggy trace.

" ' In Georgia nine negroes were arrested and chained in a warehouse on the accusation that they were suspected of burning real estate. They were all intelligent, industrious men, and declared that they could easily prove their innocence. That night they were all shot by a mob, and their widowed wives and fatherless children were driven from their homes, never to return.

" ' At Lake City, South Carolina, simply because he was appointed postmaster, a prominent negro and his little child were shot to death. His innocent wife and other children were shot and maimed for life. His home was burned above his head, while he and his dead babe were consumed by the flames.'

" Only a few days ago in Augusta, Ga., a negro was lynched for shooting in self-defense a white man who was insulting a young woman in a street car. Because the Rev. J. W. White, a negro Baptist minister, published in his paper, the *Georgia Baptist*, a paragraph quoted from a Washington paper condemning the lynching, he was mobbed by the white men of Augusta and obliged to retract his sta'ement.

" Samuel Creed Cross has investigated the facts in regard to the recent case of the burning of the negro Hose, near Atlanta, Ga., to witness which excursions were made from Atlanta. I will quote Mr. Cross' own statement : ' A white man, Crawford, was indebted to a negro by the name of Hose, and he refused to pay. They had a quarrel, wherein Crawford drew a revolver, and the negro slew him with an ax and fled. The tragic scene was in the yard where Hose was chopping wood. Mrs. Crawford was in the house, and Hose did not molest her in the least. He killed Crawford in self-defense and that is all, in spite of the countless falsehoods which pernicious prejudice is pleased to write and tell. . . . Hose was lynched and chained to a tree. His ears and fingers were cut off one by one, and handed to the howling crowd.'

" But I cannot continue the revolting descriptions of the most barbarous cruelty in recent history. You all remember the newspaper descrip:ions of the scenes of the burning of the negro Hose, a scene witnessed by a multitude of the most influential citizens of Georgia. Indeed, the words of Mr. Cross are none too strong when he says that ' this barbarity beggars the butchery of the Spanish Inquisition in her palmiest days.'

" But the lynchings of negroes in the South are not the worst outrage which the negroes suffer. The article in the *Nineteenth Century*, to which I referred, exposes the still more serious outrage of the ' convict lease system ' of the ex-slave states. How many of this audience are familiar with the workings of this system? Mr. Tobias says that it is worse than the old system of slavery, ' of which the convict lease is a relic and direct consequence.'

"Under the 'convict lease system' prisoners are leased out by the state to individual contractors, 'farmed out to the highest bidder for human flesh.' 'Prisoners are working in coal and iron mines, in sawmills, on wheat, cotton and corn farms, building railways, working in brickyards, phosphate mines and turpentine distilleries. In many of the Southern states lessees have full control of prisoners, with absolute authority to work them wherever they desire, and to administer such punishment as they see fit. They have the option of sub-leasing their victims to others who may desire cheap labor. All ages and sexes work side by side during the day and occupy the same compartments at night. Hence immorality abounds in convict camps, and the death rate is simply enormous. Women and young girls are in regular association with men and boys, and for failing to comply with some frivolous rule of the white "bosses" they are whipped in the most rude manner in the presence of men and boys.' . . . 'The guards are generally poor white men armed with Winchester rifles, and in many cases bloodhounds are kept to capture any convict who may try to escape.' . . . 'A day's work is often from sixteen to twenty hours in duration, rain or shine. Food is very poor, and clothes are scant. Prisoners of both sexes are given their raw food, which they must cook as best they can on little fires on the ground, with the ball and chain about their weary limbs. The sanitary condition in the camp is simply vile—dirt and vermin abounding. . . . Most camps in which prisoners sleep have neither bunks nor mattresses, the bare ground being the only bed. Prisoners are whipped with leather straps, getting from fifteen to fifty lashes, or as many as the white bosses choose to give them. As a result of the commingling of men and women in the camps, thousands of colored children have been born, brought up and schooled in the grossest crimes.'

"Nineteen twentieths of these prisoners, according to Mr. Cable, are negroes. Is it because the negroes are such great criminals? Not at all. It is because the negroes rarely if ever have a fair, unprejudiced trial. Says Mr. Tobias: 'It is never necessary for a white person to prove that a negro is actually guilty of any sort of offense. It is enough for a white person to allege that a negro has committed a crime, and officers are sent out to bring in the culprit, and if that particular one cannot be found, bring in any negro! Of course, the negro is guilty, whether he knows anything about the alleged offense or not, and so he must prove his innocence, which is absolutely impossible in a Southern court—or be sent to increase the prison ranks, which means a financial profit to the state and to private individuals as well.'

"Does this seem like extravagant language? Listen to these words by Mr. Cable: ' Have our opponents observed the workings of this convict lease system? To put such a system as a rod of punishment into the hands of a powerful race sitting in judgment upon the misdemeanors of a feebler and despised caste would warp the verdicts of the most righteous people under the sun. Examine our Southern penitentiary reports. What shall we say to such sentences inflicted for larceny alone as twelve, fourteen, fifteen, twenty, and in one case forty years of penal service, whose brutal tasks and whippings kill in an average of five years.' Mr. Cable specifies one sentence upon a negro of twenty years' penal servitude for ' hog stealing.' It is a commonly accepted fact that many white men are never even arrested for killing a negro. A hog has commercial value; a negro has commercial value only when he is condemned to penal servitude.

"' It is a Southern boast,' says Mr. Cross, ' that few whites are arrested and arraigned for criminality against the blacks.' If a white woman is violated by a negro in the South, the negro is straightway lynched; if a negro woman is violated by a white man, as multitudes of them are every year, a white jury will scarcely ever punish such violation.

"And this condition of things is daily growing worse and worse. At the recent white man's conference on the negro question, held at Montgomery, Ala., at one time the capital of the Confederacy, the Hon. John Temple Graves, of Georgia, emphatically declared that the white man will not permit the negro 'to have an equal part in the industrial, political, social and civil advantages of the United States;' that the negro ' will never, North or South, be permitted to govern in any state or county where he has a majority;' that he ' can never, North or South, be received in equal social and personal relations with the families of the white race.'

"At this conference the repeal of the Fifteenth Amendment to the Constitution of the United States was publicly and unblushingly advocated. In the new constitutions of Louisiana, Mississippi and South Carolina, the most iniquitous provisions are made to disfranchise the negro. A white oligarchy controls in these states to-day. When the ballot is taken away from the negro he loses more than the ballot. His legal status is affected. What imperfect rights he formerly possessed are gravely imperiled. Says John L. Love: 'The whole trend of Southern legislation is to fix what has been termed the proper status of the negro—subordination to the superior race. Not a single line has been written upon the statute books for a single Southern state within the last decade in recognition of the negro as a man entitled to respect or fair and just consideration.'

"In view of all these facts, the question at the head of my sermon to-night is an exceedingly pertinent one—'Is the negro a man?' In the freest and most democratic country of the world, a country in many respects of advanced ideals of civilization, we are obliged to sadly confess that the negro is not treated as a man. He is not a man. He is not an equal. Cruelly torn from his own country, and for 250 years enslaved by the white man's greed, he must continue to suffer for the white man's sin. It is wrong, horribly wrong! I sympathize with all my heart with the negro's indignation against the wrong, and with him I will stand as long as I live to protest against that wrong and to seek to secure for him what is his fundamental right—justice, liberty, fair play, social as well as political equality.

"My friends, if you and I possess any compassionate humanity; if you and I have shared to any extent the spirit of Jesus of Nazareth, as we profess to do; if you and I have caught but a glimpse of what is implied by the law of equal-freedom, this confession that we are obliged to make, that to-day in America the negro, no matter what may be his culture and refinement, no matter what may be his character and attainments, simply because his skin is black, nay, simply because the blood of his race flows in his veins, for he may be as white as I am,—this confession, that the negro is not a man and an equal, carries with it a very practical duty, imposes on us a very urgent responsibility.

The question is, Will we—you and I—do our duty, at whatever personal sacrifice? William Lloyd Garrison, fifty years ago, devoted himself to the noble task of the abolition of slavery. He died in 1879, fondly dreaming that his task had been accomplished. That task will never be accomplished until the negro is a man, a free man, the social and political equal of every man."

W'EN I GITS HOME

BY PAUL LAURENCE DUNBAR

It's moughty tiahsome layin' 'roun'
Dis sorrer-laden earfly groun',
An' oftentimes I thinks, thinks I,
'Twould be a sweet t'ing des to die,
    An' go 'long home.

Home whaih de frien's I loved 'll say,
"We've waited fu' you many a day,
Come hyeah an' res' yo'se'f, an' know
You's done wid sorrer an' wid woe,
    Now you's at home."

W'en I gits home some blessid day,
I 'lows to th'ow my caihs erway,
An' up an' down de shinin' street,
Go singin' sof' an' low an' sweet,
    W'en I gits home.

I wish de day was neah at han',
I's tiahed of dis grievin' lan',
I's tiahed of de lonely yeahs,
I want to des dry up my teahs,
    An' go 'long home.

Oh, Mastah, won't you sen' de call?
My frien's is daih, my hope, my all.
I's waitin' whaih de road is rough,
I want to hyeah you say, "Enough,
    Ol' man, come home!"

UNCLE MOSES WEARY OF LIFE.